Alternate Civilities

Alternate Civilities

Democracy and Culture in China and Taiwan

Robert P. Weller

BOSTON UNIVERSITY

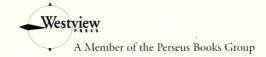

A Member of the Perseus Books Group

Copyright © 1999 by Westview Press, A Member of the Perseus Books Group

First published in 1999 in the United States of America by Westview Press, 5500 Central Avenue, Boulder, Colorado 80301-2877, and in the United Kingdom by Westview Press, 12 Hid's Copse Road, Cumnor Hill, Oxford OX2 9JJ

Published in paperback 2001.

Visit us on the World Wide Web at www.westviewpress.com

Cataloging-in-Publication Data on file with the Library of Congress.
ISBN 0-8133-3931-6 (pbk)

PERSEUS
POD
ON DEMAND   10 9 8 7 6 5 4 3 2

For Alice

Contents

Figures

Preface

Powerfully centralized political control advanced all over the world in the early-twentieth century, especially with the rise of the communist and corporatist regimes that peaked at mid-century. The end of the century, however, has brought a wave of democratization on both the right and the left. China, now alone among the old giants of all-embracing political power, still upholds its Leninist principles. This is all the more remarkable when we recall the profound economic changes of the past two decades, and China's weathering of the storms of 1989 that brought down communism elsewhere. People within China and abroad are understandably wondering what is next.

One important school of thought claims that China is unlikely to produce an open political system essentially for cultural reasons. As championed by Lee Kuan Yew of Singapore, among others, this claim rests on the idea that "Confucian culture" provides an alternative to Western civil values; this has become an important challenge to attempts to create a global human rights agenda. Some Western scholars, though fonder of civil liberties than Lee Kuan Yew, similarly focus on China's authoritarian political culture, its historical lack of any democratic institutions, and its absence of horizontal institutions of trust. They also conclude that no fundamental political change is likely there. The other important school of thought is far more optimistic about democracy, because it sees market economies of the kind China has begun to foster as pushing inexorably against Communist political control. Culture is not so much of an obstacle after all in this view of modern society; it will simply change as the economic conditions change. The argument between these two opposed views of China's future rests above all on different understandings of how culture, economy, and politics interrelate.

This book examines those relationships through just one aspect of the problem—the social groups that lie between family and state. These associations constitute the local building blocks of democratic politics, from earth god temple groups to chambers of commerce. Groups like these played a core role in Taiwan's democratization, and similar groups are developing in the People's Republic. Their potential will help to determine China's political future.

Unlike those who find no important changes in a millennium of authoritarian political culture, this book sees a very different and more promising set of political possibilities. By comparing China with the vibrant democracy that has developed over the last decade in Taiwan, I show how civil democracy can grow out of Chinese cultural roots and authoritarian institutions. By concentrating on local associational dynamics in both places, I identify spheres of informal social life with the potential to generate new forms of political life. Unlike the market triumphalists, however, I also argue that these new forms will grow out of China's own long cultural roots. We should not expect to see a "civil society" of the sort Enlightenment philosophers imagined when they first used the term.

One of the themes of this book is that modernity—in both its capitalist and socialist forms—does not destroy civil institutions either through an ever more powerful state or an ever more atomizing market individualism. There is always an informal social sector that embeds market ties and that finds the free space in any regime of state control. In repressive regimes like China and Taiwan (until recently), formally institutionalized groups with genuine independence are impossible. Locally and informally, however, indigenous cultural and social resources continue to thrive. Networks of personalistic ties, revitalization of older communal ties like religion, and ties through women are central to this process. They shape the kinds of organizations that form if the government decides, like Taiwan's, to change course.

The specific cases I take up here—business groups, religious associations, and the environmental movement—all have an informal local side and a more solidly institutionalized and larger side. One of the discoveries I made while working through these cases was the important role women often played in each of these sectors. Women's social experience in China and Taiwan is significantly different from men's, and this affects their associational lives. Women's networks often rely less on patrilineal kinship than men's, they have stronger local roots, and are often less formally organized and therefore less visible to the state. This has put them at the forefront of informal civil association—still the only kind possible in China. In the chapters that follow they will appear across the range of organizations, from rotating loan associations to raise credit for businesses, to religious healing, to environmental activism.

These local and relatively amorphous collections of social capital do not simply reproduce Western civil values; their roots lie elsewhere. Yet they can still provide a strong impetus toward democratization, as Taiwan has shown. Our usual concept of "civil society" does not fit well, but the cases I will discuss point to the possibility of an alternate civility. This is not the stubborn remnant of an ancient authoritarian culture, nor is it

the reflex of market economics. It is instead the active creation of new solutions to the problems of modern life. Taiwan has already shown the
cultural possibility of such a Chinese democracy, although it also shows
the crucial role of the state. China itself has opened up much more space
at the local, informal level over the last fifteen years. This book explores
some of the directions that process may take.

Robert P. Weller
Boston

Acknowledgments

This book is a collaboration—not in any direct sense, but as the result of a decade-long conversation with my colleagues and graduate students. It was only after finishing the manuscript that I realized how much I owed in particular to the bimonthly seminars and informal conversations at the Institute for the Study of Economic Culture at Boston University. I want to thank especially my past and present coworkers there, who stimulated so much thought: Peter Berger, Robert Hefner, Adam Seligman, Marilyn Halter, Frank Heuberger, and Laura Nash. I am equally grateful to my long partner in research and old friend, Hsin-Huang Michael Hsiao of the Institute of Sociology at the Academia Sinica in Taiwan, whose help has been so important to me. Chang Wei-an of the Department of Sociology at Ch'ing-hua University in Taiwan inspired much of the discussion of gender here, when he pointed out the implicit theme in several article manuscripts of mine. I am also, once again, deeply grateful to Stevan Adoga Harrell, for his critical comments on the manuscript.

I presented rough versions of the general argument here to the Social Sciences Research Council/American Council of Learned Societies conference on "Market Culture: Entrepreneurial Precedents and Ethical Dilemmas in East and Southeast Asia" in 1994, the conference on "Transition of Values in Civil Society" sponsored by the Club of Rome and the Bertelsmann Foundation in 1995, and at the Fairbank Center Seminar of Harvard University in 1996. My thanks to the organizers for inviting me, and to the participants for their patience and feedback.

The research on business associations benefited from funding from the Institute for the Study of Economic Culture. This allowed me to send two graduate students, Li Jiansheng and Zhang Yuehong, for a summer of interviewing in China. I am grateful to them for the valuable information they produced. I have also learned a great deal from working with Li Jiansheng and Susan McEwen on their dissertations, as will be apparent to readers of Chapter 4. I also presented a very early version of this material at the conference on "Enterprise Organization, Social Relations, and Cultural Practices in Chinese Societies," held in Taiwan in 1992. Comments received there were very helpful, especially from my discussant, Chang Wei-an.

The work on religion in Chapter 5 has been improved by my collaboration with Chien-yu Julia Huang, another graduate student here. It also profited from presentations at the international conference on "Daoist Tradition and Modernity" sponsored by the Konrad Adenauer Foundation in 1997, and at the session on "Female Religious Practice and Social Change in Contemporary East Asia" at the annual meeting of the American Anthropological Association in 1994.

For work on the environmental movement, I am grateful for the research assistance of Chien-yu Julia Huang, Li Zonglin, and Zhao Huimei, and for comments from colleagues at the Institute of Ethnology of the Academia Sinica, especially Lu Hwei-syin. Part of the research was funded by the Wenner-Gren Foundation for Anthropological Research, whose help I gratefully acknowledge. On the People's Republic of China (PRC) side, I have learned from conversations with Leslyn Hall and Evan Osnos (currently a senior at Harvard), and from many seminars through the China Project of Harvard's Committee on the Environment. Various aspects of this work benefited from presentations at the Taiwan Studies Workshop at Harvard University in 1996, the conference on "Confucianism and Ecology" at the Center for the Study of World Religions in 1996, the conference on "Taiwan, A Decade of Democratization" sponsored by George Washington University and the University of Michigan in 1996, the conference on "Reconciling Economic Growth and Environmental Protection in China" at Harvard University in 1995, the workshop on "Environmental Movements in Asia" sponsored by the Nordic Institute of Asian Studies and the International Institute of Asian Studies in Leiden in 1994, and the conference on "National Parks Interpretation and Education" sponsored by Taiwan's Ministry of the Interior in 1993.

1

Culture, Economy, and the Roots of Civil Change

China's political future concerns policymakers around the world almost as much as it does 1.2 billion Chinese citizens. Chinese societies have tried a panoply of different political systems in the course of the twentieth century. They began the century holding on to the dying remnant of the old imperial system with its emperor, magistrates, runners, and Confucian examination system. Taiwan and Hong Kong at the time were classic colonies with virtually no indigenous political power. The next few decades brought warlords, chaos in a few places, and most importantly the Republican government—economically modernizing (at least in intention), corrupt, politically authoritarian, and sometimes brutal. The Communist victory in 1949 finally brought peace, but not political stability, as the country lurched between following general Soviet policy and charging ahead into an egalitarian communism that left the Soviets panting angrily in the dust during the Great Leap Forward and then the Cultural Revolution. The really stunning recent political change has been Taiwan's move from authoritarian control to true democracy beginning in the late 1980s.

China's economic transformation as it has rediscovered markets during the same period has also brought some political loosening, but nothing like the dramatic changes in Taiwan. Yet the breadth of the recent social changes in China and the modern history of drastic political upheaval lead many, both in China and abroad, to wonder what the most appropriate and likely political structure for China will be. Two main schools and a few variants currently dominate the debates: One sees China as the latest success for an Asian-style authoritarianism that has no need or desire for Western liberal values, and another sees the triumph of market capitalism and the end of communism almost everywhere else in the world as the harbinger of a basically universal liberal social, economic, and political order.

Some sort of Asian authoritarianism seems to be the direction of choice for China's current rulers. It has considerable popular appeal as well. I was bumping along an arid and very peripheral corner of China a few years ago, sharing a Jeep with a senior professor and a young graduate student of his. The professor had suffered terribly during the Cultural Revolution, constantly humiliated and then forced to do years of bitter labor in one of the harshest and poorest environments in China. The student had grown up with the reforms. Somehow the conversation turned to Mao Zedong. The old professor, in spite of all he had been through, saw many positive contributions from the Great Helmsman, especially his vision of a new kind of China. The student disagreed at every turn, speaking with the bitterness one would have expected from someone who had actually lived through some of the worst periods. The student's idea of an attractive leader was instead Singapore's Lee Kuan Yew, one of the foremost champions of an Asian authoritarianism that rejects liberal values as Western ethnocentrism at best and neocolonialism at worst. Such a leader, he argued, could bring China wealth and stability without giving in to Western ideologies. This student was far from unusual—he was sympathetic with the "democracy" movement of 1989, concerned about the environment, and eager to study abroad. He was also eager for a China that could be strong and respected in the world by its own standards.

This image of an economic superpower morally opposed to the West has been very upsetting to a range of outsiders, from human rights groups opposed to political arrests, to U.S. congress members trying to slow trade with China.[1] It is not hard to imagine a virulent combination of economic strength (based on simple projections of recent growth rates), political reaction (as in the powerful clampdown after 1989 and continuing calls for renewed Party control and education in socialist values), and nationalism (seen now in occasional outbursts like some sporting events, the conflict over the Nansha/Spratley Islands, and books like the influential *China Can Say No*).[2] It is no accident that two recent influential American books on foreign policy close with purely imaginary wars between the United States and China.[3]

The major alternative people discuss is China's move more fully into a global modernity based on liberal market economics and democratic politics. The transformation of Eastern Europe and the ex-Soviet Union and the new wave of democratization in parts of Latin America and Africa imply for some the inevitable demise of socialist politics like China's. This would be, in Fukuyama's famous phrase, the "end of history."[4] Taiwan is the most relevant example here. By the mid-1950s, when both Taiwan and the mainland had recovered from their long wars, they had very similar cultural traditions, single-party states constructed on Leninist models, and powerful authoritarian control over daily life. They differed, of course, in the path of economic development they would pursue in the coming decades. Taiwan's thriving market economy ultimately helped push the island to full democracy. China's bullish new economy is headed in the same direction, making for plausible speculation that the political system could change in the same way.

While many in the West, and some in China, deeply desire such a change, it too contains an ugly variation—that the end of authoritarian central control would bring chaos and corruption, democracy to the point of anarchy. Severe social problems in much of Eastern Europe and the bloody collapse of Yugoslavia make this scenario quite plausible to many in China. Talk of Tibetan or Taiwanese independence, and even inklings of Cantonese chauvinism or other revivals of strongly local sentiment, only add to the fear of a general breakdown of central authority. Unified political power in China, after all, has collapsed many times in the past, sometimes for centuries at a time.

Culture and Economy

Understanding the dynamics behind these possibilities is central to the welfare of everyone in China and Taiwan, and also to formulating effective policies toward China. Does one promote a human rights agenda, for example, by encouraging trade to foster independent business interests, or by punitively limiting trade to send a message to the government? Can there be an Asian civil society, or even an Asian modernity, that retains values fundamentally different from those that developed in Enlightenment Europe?

Most of the reasoning behind various expectations for China's future has relied on two major factors: Chinese (or Asian) culture as a push to authoritarian politics and the market as a motor of change toward values of individualism and civil liberties. At heart this is an argument between two opposed views of how culture relates to economic change. In the "ancient curse" theory of culture, some remote ancestor becomes burdened with a worldview (usually called Confucianism in this case), after which it is inexorably passed down from generation to generation.[5] Changing economics are largely irrelevant, and politics is a product of the cultural past. The "Etch-A-Sketch" theory of culture is the opposite. Here, as with the toy, you can draw any culture you want. When your interests require a new one, you just give a little shake and start over. Markets thus drive changing values in this view, and historical legacies do not count for much. I simplify sometimes complex arguments here, of course, and it is worth taking a closer look at the cases that have been made for both sides.

A Culture of Authority?

The argument that Chinese societies are unlikely to produce an open political system largely for cultural reasons comes in both Asian and Western forms. The Asian form was championed initially by Lee Kuan Yew, currently Singapore's senior minister, and Mohamad Mahatir, prime minister of Malaysia. It has become quite influential in China, and internationally is one of the most important voices opposing universalist values of civil liberties. The argument, at least in its Chinese form, rests on the idea that "Confucian culture" provides an alternative to Western ideas of human rights. Here the family metaphors of paternal benevolence and filial respect are extended to the nation as a whole, in a move that recalls both the European corporatist ideologies of Franco or Salazar (always the champions of the family) and Confucius himself.

In Singapore, this has evolved out of a largely unsuccessful Confucian education campaign into an ideology of shared values that allegedly unite the island's Chinese, Malay, and Indian populations: nation before community and society above self, the family as the basic social unit, consensus over contention as a way of resolving issues, community support and respect for the individual, and harmony among racial and religious groups.[6] The roots of this lie partly in an authoritarian reading of Confucianism, with the central government as caring father to a family of obedient children-citizens. This is hardly the only possible reading of Confucius, but it is consistent with the philosophy's use by two millennia of imperial Chinese governments.

This attempt to foster new Asian values also partly reacts against a rather occidentalized reading of "Western" morality, which is said to privilege individual over community and nation, dissolve family and religious morality into self-serving careerism, and solve problems through adversarial competition alone. The state's goal is to avoid the moral degeneration and social chaos for which politicians like Lee Kuan Yew constantly lambaste the United States and democratic Asian governments like Taiwan. Even the token recognition of the individual in this system is contextualized in a broader community. These were the ideas championed by Singapore, Malaysia, Indonesia, Iran, and China at the UN World Conference on Human Rights in 1993 as an alternative to Western concepts of human rights based on civil liberties.

Such values claim to be naturally independent from the global market economy, which advocates of Asian values typically embrace wholeheartedly. Campaigns for stepped-up "spiritual civilization" in the Peo-

ple's Republic of China (PRC) similarly assume that the nation can develop a market economy without taking the "spiritually corrupt" Western values that historically grew up with that economy. This is a singu-
larly un-Marxist point of view, of course, where culture has a life fully
independent from the economy. Yet it has been important in the People's
Republic all along—the theoretical underpinning of the Cultural Revolution was also the idea that culture could remain stubbornly feudal or
bourgeois even when the economic systems underlying those cultures
had been utterly destroyed. This was an ancient curse indeed.

The Western, mostly scholarly, version of a determining Chinese authoritarian culture points to many of these same values. Instead of embracing them as a normative alternative, however, Western scholars generally regret how such values make a democratic China impossible. One
of the pioneers in studies of Chinese political culture, Lucian Pye, identified a number of key characteristics that have been continuous through
imperial and modern history. These include the centrality of hierarchy, a
pervasive concern with morality over bureaucratic machinery (and thus
of rule of men over rule of law), an imperative of conformity, and an an-
tipathy toward the individual.[7] Pye does not share Lee Kuan Yew's enthusiasm for any of this, but instead sees it as a key explanation of Chinese factionalism and periodic crises of authority. Like the "Asian
values" enthusiasts, though, Pye has a very robust version of culture, in
his case based in socialization practices, which has lasted China through
the ages and shows little sign of any fundamental change.[8]

A related argument stresses the lack of institutional guarantees of trust
in China. The Chinese skill at using interpersonal relations and forging
personal networks of connections, according to this argument, evolved
largely as a response to the absence of larger social or political mechanisms that could create the trust needed to do business. Such networks
have turned out to be very useful in fostering dynamic family businesses
in modern economies. Yet seeing this as an inherent feature of all Chinese
societies makes it very difficult to imagine China building a democracy,
when the only available social resources are particularistic personal ties
and the authoritarian state.[9]

Political scientists outside the China field have also discovered culture,
and nearly always prefer the ancient curse version. Robert Putnam's important study of political variation in Italy also looks at social trust as an
explanation for the relatively democratic society of the north and the relatively autocratic one of the south. Already six hundred years ago, he argues, northern Italy was characterized by horizontal ties of trust and mutual assistance, while the south emphasized vertical ties of hierarchy.[10]
The situation has been self-perpetuating ever since, leading to current
political differences. Samuel Huntington has recently taken an even

stronger culturalist position, chopping the world into seven or eight "civilizations," defined culturally with a strong emphasis on religion. Nearly all of these have existed for a millennium or more, apparently unchanged in their fundamentals. With the end of the Cold War, he predicts, the world will return to its older lines of unbreachable difference, and the potentials for major conflict lie along his civilizational fault lines. Possible conflict between the "West" and the "Sinic" world play a large role in this analysis.

His version of the "Confucian ethos" stresses "the values of authority, hierarchy, the subordination of individual rights and interests, the importance of consensus, the avoidance of confrontation, 'saving face,' and, in general, the supremacy of the state over society and of society over the individual."[11] If this sounds rather like Singapore's version of things, it is because Huntington, more than nearly any other important Western observer, is sympathetic to their "ambitious and enlightened" effort to create a regional cultural identity.[12] He is less cynical than others about this ideology being a convenient rationalization by an authoritarian government, largely because he agrees that such things are natural for the Sinic civilization, and because he sees no real possibility for fundamental change.

These strong cultural analyses tend to look past the case of a truly thriving Chinese democracy that already exists—Taiwan. The Kuomintang (KMT) government that took over Taiwan in 1945 learned its political organization hand-in-hand with the Communist Party. As on the mainland today, the government would not tolerate any institutionalization of public opinion outside of its control. Just like the mainland, all kinds of horizontal ties in fact existed (religion, fictive and real kinship, rotating credit associations), but they had no chance to grow. When I first lived in Taiwan in the late 1970s the similarities to my images of the People's Republic were stunning. Walls were painted with political slogans, television stations carried quotes from President Chiang Kai-shek, and the press was so tightly controlled that even *Time* and *Newsweek* regularly showed the black marks of the censor.

One could have argued around 1980, as Singapore argues now, that Chinese political culture simply preferred paternalistic, authoritarian control to democracy.[13] Nor was this just an official government line. I often heard Taiwanese villagers criticize the United States for having too much freedom and not enough respect for authority: Was it true that we all carry guns? Was it true that we charge our aged parents rent if they come to visit? They were generally more polite than Lee Kuan Yew, but the message was roughly the same.

That is why the lifting of martial law on July 15, 1987, offers such an important lesson. Within months, Taiwan had a nationally organized environmental movement, women's movement, and labor movement.[14] Each of these movements has continued to thrive and grow. Taiwan's newspapers, for example, documented just ten cases of environmental demonstrations in 1981, but there were 278 a decade later.[15] Many of these involved island-wide environmental organizations, which continue to thrive. Within the next few years, Taipei also developed new institutions of public gathering, from discos (and now karaoke television or KTV parlors) to beer halls to revived tea houses. By 1996 there were also almost 14,000 registered nongovernmental organizations (NGOs) and foundations.[16] Singapore now points to Taiwan as a place with too much freedom, and most Taiwanese explicitly reject Singapore's version of "Asian values."

Taiwan does not simply disprove the cultural explanation. Its century of effective independence from the mainland, fifty years of colonial rule from Japan, and very different economic system considerably complicate the comparison. Nevertheless, Taiwan demands a more nuanced consideration of cultural change than is usual among people arguing about authoritarian culture in Asia. No simple monolithic notion of an authoritarian Chinese or Asian culture will explain what has happened there.

Taiwan has not abandoned Chinese culture—this is clear to anyone who has spent significant amounts of time there. In fact there is something of a cultural renaissance going on, with everything from a religious revival to tea houses to a new Confucianism developing in opposition to Lee Kuan Yew's. In the chapters that follow I will argue that culture has in fact been important in Taiwan's political change, but only because Chinese culture is, and has always been, multifaceted and adaptable. As an anthropologist I tend to take a worm's-eye view of society, from the bottom up. One of the advantages of this is the ability to see a whole range of cultural variation in both China and Taiwan, including the alternatives to authoritarianism that thrive in the free spaces it always leaves. Chinese culture, indeed any culture, is not the monolith that Huntington carves out.

Markets as the Motor of History?

The Etch-A-Sketch theory of culture is not so troubled by China's alleged authoritarian culture. Cultures can change, after all, and the apparent ongoing globalization of culture and economy during the twentieth century argues against any cultural determinism. The most powerful versions of this argument point out how values like individualism and the rule of law are implied by a capitalist market economy. Such an economy fosters a bourgeoisie with interests in lobbying the government, creates a complex division of labor that is harder for a government to control, and increases levels of wealth and education in the society.[17] All of this, in theory at least, should encourage movement toward democracy. The events of 1989 (outside of China) were enough to allow some to declare victory for this vision of a liberal economic and political triumph and an "end to history" for arguments about the ultimate vision of society.[18]

In fact, several quite different lines of general theory about capitalism and culture led us to expect a global cultural homogenization accompanying economic development. The modernization theory that thrived in the 1960s, for example, tried to generalize Weber's argument about the Protestant ethic to all societies, looking for a functional equivalent to the rationalizing work ethic as a precondition for capitalist development, and for the simultaneous development of civil institutions and ideas. Thus, in a spectacularly unsuccessful prediction, many expected Chinese East Asia to be a developmental disappointment. The "enchanted garden" of Chinese religion was thought to discourage ascetic secular rationalization, while family-centered particularism impeded effective economic decisions and broader ties of trust.[19] If countries like China were to develop successfully, however, all would eventually have to recreate similar features—a single culture of capitalism that was secular, rationalizing and civil. In this view the market comes in like a massive glacier, fundamentally reshaping the cultural landscape according to its own dynamic, and largely erasing what was there before. The only alternative, apparently, is a culture so immune to change that modernization is impossible. Eventually all cases of modernization develop a shared market culture, including some form of liberal democracy.[20]

The picture of a global liberal economic and political victory, painted so rosily by some, has an ugly side. Market economies appear to sap the life from traditional values whenever they begin to dominate social relations. Enthusiasts may praise this as the rise of motivated individuals, but critics see only calculation and greed. Whatever their view of the result, social scientists have been exploring the change at least since Marx on alienation, Durkheim on anomie, and Weber on the iron cage of capitalism and the "unprecedented inner loneliness of the single individual" standing directly beneath the hard gaze of God.[21] All three, in spite of the enormous differences among them, led us to expect a modern market culture of individualism, secularism, and rationality (in Weber's sense of maximizing control and efficiency), and all three also made us aware of the enormous cultural costs of this transition.[22]

Deeply connected social communities tend to break down, and many kinds of relationships, once rich in social meaning, become reduced to market transactions. Even core social relations of family life like food preparation and child care are subject to constant pressure from the market economy to become just more commodities. Marx and Engels expected capitalism ultimately to destroy the family through this process, just as Weberians predicted a thorough secularization and loss of religious values. Examples of how people undergoing a market transition perceive a loss of values are easy to find. English peasants would riot when their moral expectations of "just" prices were not met by traders willing to answer only to markets.[23] Malaysian peasants have resisted just the same processes—the end of a precapitalist moral economy—in the twentieth century.[24] Michael Taussig's analysis of Colombian peasants shows their incarnation of this problem as devil worship, as men who profit from the wage economy are said to have sold their souls (or the souls of babies) to the devil.[25]

Yet this vision of the market as juggernaut running over all earlier culture, resisted but ultimately unstoppable, is just as overdrawn as the image of culture as ancient curse. Markets do indeed put pressure on families and religion, but both have managed to thrive anyway under modernity. Even the United States has not collapsed into extreme individualism, nor is it likely to do so. Market economies, like nonmarket economies, require social capital to function; they cannot afford to erase all ties larger than the individual but smaller than the state.[26] In addition, people everywhere have reacted to the pressures of market culture partly by embracing the new opportunities (not everyone does well in nonmodern economies after all), and partly by reacting against them. I will develop these points further below, especially in Chapter 5 on religion. For now I simply want to note that much of the world now embraces market economics but hopes to reject the values that appear to come along, and that this is part of the general reaction against the pressures of modernity everywhere. The Singapore/China version of Asian values is just such a reaction, where the evils of individualism and social chaos are said to come from the West rather than from the internal dynamics of the market.

A strong rejection of "Western" values, as in Singapore or Iran, is only one of many possible forms of a search for alternate values. Even Confucianism offers some possibilities quite different from what Lee Kuan Yew has in mind. Some Taiwanese and overseas Chinese intellectuals, for example, advance a more democratic vision of Confucius that they claim cuts through the imperial accretions of the last two millennia. They criticize the Singapore version as a remnant of the worst in the old tradition, and look back to the original Confucian texts for a truer version of the philosopher. One recent, if rather polemical Taiwanese version argues for an ecological democracy inherent in classical Confucianism that will "ward off the post-industrial ill of economic technological hegemony, where a person is just a button in a machine, economic or otherwise— easily pushed on and off, easily replaced."[27]. It goes on to say that:

Hegemony by technocrats and multi-national corporations—where only money and machines talk—grows in an ideological soil ("Western democracy") where everyone is indifferently equal in a lonely crowd, a mass society. Confucian democracy dissolves this danger. Here everyone is treasured as a social person, that is, not as a faceless individual but as a person in a specific role which is imbued with the special warmth of that particular person.[28]

This is a clear example of the concern with alternatives to an atomized Western market culture on the one hand, and to an authoritarian Confucianism on the other. As with earlier generations of Confucianisms, this one is largely confined to intellectuals, and neither this nor the Singapore version much qualifies as popular culture. Other ideas play comparable roles outside intellectual circles, as I will discuss in the chapters that follow.

Is there in fact one universal market culture—with its implied civil liberties and political democracy—or are there many? Are features like individualism, rationality, and secularism (or, for the critics, selfishness, greed, and godlessness) inherent to the experience of capitalist markets? Does a world market imply cultural convergence in politics and economics, or can some earlier systems manage to forge unique versions of capitalism or democracy? Empirically the case is still open, at least for Chinese East Asia. The system continues to transform even as we watch it; family ties, for example, appear less important in business than they did even a decade ago (see Chapter 4). The evidence does suggest, however, that capitalist markets exert comparable pressures everywhere in the world, but that local systems react differently to those pressures. The result is often a complex split, with some cultural developments indeed trending toward some kind of global, liberal market culture, while others counter that trend. The Chinese cases, I will argue, do not support a simple convergence toward a universal culture, but neither do they show a clear Confucian riposte. Instead, they experience an ongoing tension between value and market, community and individual. This tension itself constitutes a shared feature of market modernity. The ways in which people resolve this tension, or at least hold it under control, on the other hand, vary widely even within a single society.[29]

In particular, many areas of life outside the economy undergo increasing pressure as market rationality pushes beyond the marketplace itself. Battle lines may be drawn in many places across a society between a utilitarian/rationalist tendency, and traditionalist or moralist alternatives. Certainly the history of the West has not been the triumphant march of the market over everything else. The nineteenth-century religious entrenchment against the Enlightenment still echoes today in attacks on secular humanism. In art and literature, the Romantics provided one of the precursors to modern environmentalism. Twentieth-century pressures toward making traditional family functions like child care or food preparation into commodities have been met by a vigorous defense (or perhaps invention) of traditional family values.

Comparing China and Taiwan

In their extreme forms the ancient curse theory of culture tells us that China will never be democratic, and the Etch-A-Sketch theory that it will inevitably democratize. The challenge is to come up with a more realistic, empirically based understanding of the situation. This will involve taking culture seriously, unlike the kind of market triumphalism that sees capitalism remaking all cultures in its own Western image. But it will also involve taking markets seriously, with their powerful effects on interests and values. Human beings can think and strategize, and that ultimately makes culture subject to change.

The empirical case is greatly aided by the existence of Taiwan: A full-blown democracy now exists there, but one whose social base is still identifiably Chinese, as I will argue in the chapters that follow. A comparison of China and Taiwan is as close to a natural experiment as the social sciences can come. The great majority of Taiwan's population came over in various waves from mainland China beginning in the seventeenth century. Almost all of these were from a narrow band along the southeast coast, including southern Fujian and northern Guangdong, until the post-1949 influx of refugees from all over the country. Even though Taiwan was a distant periphery at the beginning of this period and underwent decades of Dutch and Japanese rule, it remains culturally Chinese. Even today, after a century of nearly continuous political separation between Taiwan and the mainland, southern Fujian feels much more like Taiwan than like northern China. Similar temples are devoted to the same deities, the language is the same, people even like the same snacks. Taiwanese dialects have a few more Japanese loan words, and people are a little more likely to eat sashimi or watch sumo wrestlers on television. Taiwanese family structure, business organization, religion, interpersonal relations, and all the rest may now constitute a unique variation of Chinese culture, but no one would mistake them for anything else.

Taiwan is crucial exactly because it shows how a place can remain culturally Chinese while it develops a democratic political structure. Taiwanese have not simply been the tool of Western governments in this, or the pawns of the global media. They have reshaped their society using cultural resources available to them as they reacted to both market dynamics and international political pressures. China need not evolve the same way, of course, but if we are trying to determine its cultural potentials, the Taiwan case looms large. It shows that we can talk about alternative democracies, just as it (and Japan) showed earlier that there are alternative paths to economic modernity.

Voluntary Associations and Civil Life

I first lived in Taiwan during the late 1970s, when the authoritarian power of the state seemed unquestioned except by a small group of dissidents. I left in early 1979, just a few months after the United States broke diplomatic relations with Taiwan, and a few weeks before the high-profile arrest of several leading dissidents that resulted in long sentences to prison labor. When I went back again in 1986 I paid a visit to my old landlord in the town of Sanxia. "Things have really changed for the better in the last few years," he said. "Come on, I have to show you something." Mystified, I sat on the back of his motorcycle as we rode to what turned out to be a baseball game between two local village teams.

I asked what made this so significant. He said that the government used to forbid organized adult baseball, and encouraged people to play basketball instead. "We Taiwanese are short. We're no good at basketball, but those mainlanders [the government] wouldn't let us play baseball. Mainlanders are taller and they're better at basketball. Now things have really loosened up." I knew that the government had never allowed organized adult baseball, even though their Little League teams are perennial world powers. In the 1970s people told me that the government considered adult baseball too frivolous. In fact there were probably two more crucial reasons. The first was that baseball is so important in Japan, and the government was constantly concerned to limit what they saw as close ties between Taiwan and their old enemy Japan. The second is that baseball teams, harmless as they may look, are an example of social self-organization independent of the state, and therefore potentially dangerous no matter how frivolous their ostensible purpose.[30] The sprouting of baseball teams, along with countless other kinds of local self-organization in the 1980s, was a sign of the fundamental changes that were in progress.

Between Family and State

This book concentrates on just this kind of self-organized voluntary group intermediate between family and state. Several recent authors have considered such voluntary associations to be crucial for both economic and political development. These institutions constitute a kind of "social capital" based on horizontal ties of trust.[31] They constitute a public sphere where individuals and groups interact to influence the publicly shared understandings that govern interrelationships in collective life. Like baseball teams, they need not have explicit political goals—they still help to define society as a separate entity, to create ties among people, and to define identity. A fairly large literature has examined how market economies are embedded in such ties.[32] A smaller and more recent set of works puts these horizontal ties at the heart of stable democracy as well.[33] They point out that strong horizontal ties foster networks of trust, which in turn facilitate social coordination (including both economic functions like raising capital and political ones like organizing parties), and decrease incentives for corruption and opportunism. On the other hand, an absence of social trust encourages a powerful state to take over these functions, from increased police control to running state-owned companies.

Intermediate institutions buffer the twin threats that have rattled the twentieth century: the unremitting pressure toward rationalized totality through state and bureaucracy, and the endless dissolution into individuality. On the one hand the twentieth century has seen the creation of ever more powerful states. Doctrines of efficiency, economies of scale, and mass production that began in American factories ended up, in part, as Lenin's inspiration for socialism as a single huge Taylorist enterprise, with the workers choreographed for maximum production. Even more benign modern states intervene in daily life in ways that earlier states simply could not manage. A reaction against totalizing states accompanies this trend. Even many in the United States, which has a relatively laissez-faire state, react fervently against any perceived aggrandizement of state power. On the other hand, we also fear the increased individual atomization that has come with modernity, and look to save our families, churches, and communities from anomic dissipation. The two trends are closely related: a society of isolated individuals, one with no more unity than potatoes in the same sack (as Marx said about the French peasantry), both needs and is vulnerable to a totalizing state in ways that a more self-organizing society is not. Voluntary institutions between family and state thus play an important mediating role.

This argument lies at the heart of Putnam's recent lament that Americans increasingly go bowling alone, that America's current "democratic disarray may be linked to a broad and continuing erosion of civil engagement."[34] He is building, of course, on Tocqueville's much earlier argument that the strength of American democracy lies exactly in the proliferation of voluntary organizations.[35] A related claim has also been made for Eastern Europe's radical changes in 1989. There, the argument runs, a renaissance of civil organization from below ultimately forced political changes on the state. These organizations included a workers' union in Poland, the Church in several countries, arts organizations, and the family itself. In some cases, even corporatist mass organizations could develop a will of their own, as in Poland where "despite the grip of the party and restrictions on political expression within them, these groups provided a significant means for collective activity. Even though political aspects were ordinarily invisible or ignored, what mattered in subjective terms was the possibility of action and the promotion of private or group interests against the authorities. Many of these groups, especially professional organizations, transformed themselves into dissident bodies in the 1980s."[36]

In Taiwan various forms of social association have played direct and indirect roles in the pursuit of a collective consensus on the island's future development. These include business groups, groups pushing for various forms of empowerment (e.g., to promote rights of consumers, labor, women, indigenous peoples, environment, etc.), and new forms of religious organization. These organizations proliferated wildly after martial law was lifted in 1987.[37] For almost a decade before that, however, their precursors—a consumers' rights group, the beginnings of environmental activism, business clubs, and even baseball teams—helped promote the changes that would come. These groups were never explicitly political, but nevertheless encouraged political change. In mainland China, while market activities independent of government control have multiplied, old forms of associations have been revived, and new types of business corporations, professional groups, and social associations are growing apace. While all these need not imply a necessary process of democratization, they do constitute a kind of social capital with important implications for the future.

Voluntary Association and Civil Society

Many readers will by now have noticed that I have studiously avoided the term "civil society" while writing about many of its core issues. The term "civil society" comes with a set of problematic theoretical assumptions and historical connotations, which have strong roots in a particular European philosophical tradition. The concept of civil society grows from Enlightenment ideas of a sphere of autonomous individual activity, independent from both the state and the fetters of older kinship and feudal ties.[38] As it developed through Hegel and Marx, the market-based economy became the prime example of a civil sphere, where private interests were articulated in relation to the public sphere of the state. Developed through Tocqueville, the concept focused more on the role of self-organizing civil organizations.[39] In either case, the simultaneous growth of a philosophy of individualism was critical to the idea of a civil society, which pointed to a new form of social organization no longer dependent on premodern social ties like kinship or community, and which was also seen as independent from the state.

To fulfill the usual standards of "civil society" these intermediate associations should: (1) be voluntary, that is, based on the free choice of autonomous individuals; (2) act with civility, that is, accept the rights of others to disagree (thus ruling out organizations like gangsters); and (3) respect the legitimacy of the state while in turn enjoying a free space for action guaranteed by the state.[40] This definition distinguishes modern civil organizations from earlier forms of organization based on particularistic ties (like lineage-run schools in China, for instance) or on ties directly to the state. It also makes clear that not every voluntary organization between family and state is civil—neither revolutionary cells nor the Ku Klux Klan are examples of civil society. Organizations in a civil society may compete and disagree with each other or with the state, but all must also accept some minimal ground rules.

Is such a concept useful outside Western Europe and the United States, where it developed? Is it even useful in those places after several centuries of rapid social change? While a new enthusiasm for the idea of civil society has grown since the transformation of Eastern Europe in the 1980s, new criticisms also abound. Adam Seligman, for example, points to the roots of the concept in early eighteenth-century ideas of moral community that have simply dissolved in the last two hundred years. "Civil society" has again become an important intellectual force recently, but as an anachronism, he implies, it needs fundamental revision to work in the modern world.[41] From a different point of view, anthropologists have stressed that various communal kinds of ties are in fact not so very incompatible with civil society, and may always have been important in real civil ties, as opposed to philosophical abstractions.[42]

The events of 1989 in China and Eastern Europe caused a minor stampede of Western China-scholars looking to identify the "sprouts" of civil society in Chinese tradition, or to blame the failure of the student movement on the lack of such traditions. The literature on China has already split on this issue, with one faction arguing that a Habermasian public sphere existed (even if it was not quite a civil society), and the other seeing the Chinese stuck with a hopelessly authoritarian political culture (see Chapter 2). While I take these cultural roots very seriously, this literature tends to forget that culture is not immobile. It lives in a dialogue with social life, through which it is both reproduced and transformed. Whatever one concludes about the cultural potentials for civil society in late imperial China, it will be important to take a close look at the enormous transformations of the last century.

These organizations between family and state in China and Taiwan are not civil society in the classic sense, if such a thing ever existed. They are too strongly rooted in local, communal ties. In addition, we cannot simply assume the relevance of a dichotomy between state and society, which lies at the root of Western definitions of civil society. These are the primary reasons that I will continue to avoid "civil society" as a term. Yet there certainly were broad-based horizontal institutions, they have been central in Taiwan's democratic transition, and they have important implications for China today. There are more ways to achieve a "democratic civility" than simple reproduction of the Western history of civil society.[43]

Gender and the View from Below

Most of the literature on democratization looks at political and military elites. This concentration on the central state is helpful in at least two senses: First, these leaders are critical to maintaining a system or to changing its direction. Second, a state's leaders can deal with independent social forces in different ways, for example by incorporating social groups, by repressing them, or by carrying on a dialog with them. State structures and the decisions of top leaders have a great deal to do with Taiwan's transition to democracy and the People's Republic's retention of authoritarian control. Yet democracy also has to grow from the ground up. Even the most democratically minded political leaders (indeed especially those leaders) cannot force people into a political structure that requires social self-mobilization unless the people have the social and cultural capacity to do so. That is why I will be concerned here primarily with local life and local social organization as they articulate with a broader politics.

Cultural particularities also often show up much more clearly at the local level than in national political or social organizations. As I discuss in Chapter 6, for example, the Taiwanese environmental movement looks quite Western at its top levels. In fact, however, Taiwanese environmentalism cannot be reduced to a case of simple globalization. Local environmental organizations there have strong connections to Taiwanese religion, kinship, and gender relations, and differ significantly from the views of national environmental leaders. The variations that always existed in Chinese culture—between regions, classes, genders, ethnic groups, and all the rest—become clear only from a very local focus. Examining the possibility of multiple modernities, of indigenous paths to market success and democratic civility, requires an understanding of this local dynamic. Keeping our analytic feet on the ground will clarify how shared market pressures need not lead to shared values, even within Chinese society.

Gender provides one of the most important lines of variation in the chapters that follow. My interest in the gender dynamic of these issues is not driven by any of the theories I have been discussing. On the contrary, women have tended to be invisible in nearly all of these discussions. The concentration on political and economic behavior of central elites has in part discouraged people from looking at gender issues, because men are the most obvious actors at this level.[44] Yet in doing the research at the local level for the main topics of this book—business development, religious revivals, and social movements—I was struck at each stage by the central role that women play. As I discovered, women are both active in these changes and often different from their husbands, fathers, and sons.

This empirical result probably should not have been as surprising as I found it. Women and men, particularly in Chinese society, have had strongly differentiated roles and life experiences. Women and men are yin and yang, passive and active, inside and outside. Inside/outside was particularly relevant—the seclusion of women did not reach the extremes of some Islamic societies, but women's place was emphatically in the home. Women typically married into their husband's villages and families, thus leaving their natal families for a life among strangers. The result, as I will discuss in the following chapter, was that women created a separate social world, through their sons (whose birth gave women status in their new families), through continuing ties to their natal families, and through new ties to other women of the village. The male ideology of an infinite line of male descendants was far less important to women than these more immediate bonds of social life.[45]

In the twentieth century these ties have evolved into a kind of informal local politics where women often play a crucial role, even if they become invisible at the highest centers of power. A female-dominated Buddhist charitable group, for example, is the largest civil organization in Taiwan, with a welfare budget higher than the city of Taipei. Women are also very active in local environmentalism, but again sound rather different from their husbands. In authoritarian regimes where open social organizing of any kind may be suspect, we might expect that women's absence from more formally organized groups would give special importance to their informal networks. This importance seems to have translated into an important role for women under the new circumstances in Taiwan.

The next chapter begins to examine organizational life from below with some thoughts about the legacy of imperial China for voluntary organizations today. Contrary to what has frequently been asserted, China had many kinds of social ties between family and state.[46] While they did not constitute a civil society, they do provide resources that shape the processes changing China and Taiwan today, including various kinds of informal ties among women. Chapter 3 turns to the problem of maintaining horizontal ties of trust under the kinds of authoritarian regime that have ruled both China and Taiwan for most of the twentieth century. Again in contrast to some images, especially of the People's Republic as a case of successful totalitarian rule, the evidence points to a continued survival of intermediate social ties in spite of, and sometimes even because of, heavy-handed state efforts at totalizing control.

Each of the chapters that follow takes up very different kinds of voluntary association as they have evolved in China and Taiwan over the last few decades. Chapter 4 looks at business organizations, from the use of networks of personal relations to formal business associations like Chambers of Commerce. Both China and Taiwan show the importance of interpersonal trust in economic life (as in the rotating credit networks often run by women), but the comparison also clarifies the powerful role the state can play in shaping the social consequences of horizontal ties. These ties make it clear that voluntary civil associations may be necessary for a democratic transition, but they are no guarantee that one will occur.

Chapter 5 examines indigenous religion, which is coming back powerfully in the People's Republic and thriving like never before in Taiwan. Local religious organization shows clearly the inevitable split in market cultures: on the one hand it is happily commercializing, celebrating individuality, and encouraging profit, while on the other hand it is reacting against a perceived loss of values by offering moral alternatives. The specific form these groups take again has strong roots in earlier Chinese culture, and the resulting civil organizations thus will not simply reproduce the kinds of groups that developed in North America or Western Europe. Women's religious groups in particular have thrived in Taiwan, but in ways that do not just reiterate Western developments.

Chapter 6 examines groups involved in social movements, with most attention focused on environmental issues. Here Taiwan looks very different from the mainland, largely due to the proliferation of such groups after martial law was lifted. Yet China also has both local environmental demonstrations and national environmental NGOs. Both cases together help generate a typology of civil associations based on how formally organized they are and how voluntary membership is. The result in both China and Taiwan is a deep split between national-level associations (formalized and completely voluntary) and local movements (usually informal and more communal); local movements also tend to be realized differently across gender lines. The typology also clarifies forms of state control, with some types fairly easy to control from above and others fundamentally beyond control.

At the broadest level my argument is first that modernity does not destroy civil institutions either through an ever more powerful state or an ever more atomizing individualism. There is always an informal social sector that embeds market ties and that finds the free space in any regime of state control. Second, these kinds of horizontal ties need not reproduce "civil society" in the West, but can still provide a strong impetus toward democratization, as Taiwan has shown. Third, the idea of split market cultures clarifies how culture continues to be a force in shaping the form of these organizations without falling into either the ancient curse or the Etch-A-Sketch simplification. Fourth, women have consistently played a leading role in these horizontal organizations, which relates both to their earlier roles at home and to their structural position in modernizing states.

Ultimately all of this speaks to the possibility of democratic transformation in China. Taiwan has already shown the cultural possibility of such a change, and the chapters that follow take up the social possibilities. They also make clear, however, the crucial role of the state itself. The ability of Chinese society to self-organize will depend on the state allowing enough free space. The way the state incorporates horizontal institutions makes a crucial difference. China has in fact opened up much more space at the local, informal level over the last fifteen years. The problem for policy, which I take up at the end of the book, is how to encourage that process.

Notes

1. See, for example, Richard Bernstein and Ross H. Munro, *The Coming Conflict with China* (New York: Knopf, 1997), p. 61.

2. Song Qiang, Zhang Zangzang, Qiao Bian, et al., *Zhongguo Keyi Shou Bu: Lengzhan Hou Shidai de Zhengzhi yu Qinggan Jueze [China Can Say No: Political and Emotional Choices in the Post–Cold War Era]* (Beijing: Zhonghua Gongshang Lianhe Chunbanshe, 1996).

3. Samuel P. Huntington, *The Clash of Civilizations and the Remaking of World Order* (New York: Simon & Schuster, 1996); Bernstein and Munro, *The Coming Conflict with China.*

4. Francis Fukuyama, "The End of History?" *The National Interest* 16 (Summer 1989), pp. 3–18.

5. The "ancient curse" metaphor comes from Peter L. Berger.

6. For a summary of this evolution, see John Wong, "Promoting Confucianism for Socioeconomic Development: The Singapore Experience," and Eddie C. Y. Kuo, "Confucianism as Political Discourse in Singapore: The Case of an Incomplete Revitalization Movement," both in Wei-ming Tu, ed., *Confucian Traditions in East Asian Modernity* (Cambridge, Mass.: Harvard University Press, 1996), pp. 277–293, 294–309.

7. His classic exposition of this was in *The Spirit of Chinese Politics*, rev. ed. (Cambridge, Mass.: Harvard University Press, 1992 [1968]). Later elaborations include *The Mandarin and the Cadre: China's Political Cultures* (Ann Arbor, Mich.:

Center for Chinese Studies, University of Michigan, 1988), and "The State and the Individual: An Overview Interpretation," *China Quarterly* (September 1991), pp. 443–466.

8. More recently, Richard Bernstein and Ross H. Munro (*The Coming Conflict with China*, p. 15) have made a similar argument that democracy is "contrary to the Chinese political culture . . . [which] has never in its history operated on any notion of the consent of the governed or the will of the majority."

9. See S. Gordon Redding, "'Thickening' Civil Society: The Impact of Multinationals in China," *Development and Democracy* 11 (1996), 21–28; and Francis Fukuyama, *Trust: Social Virtues and the Creation of Prosperity* (New York: Free Press, 1995).

10. Robert D. Putnam, *Making Democracy Work: Civic Traditions in Modern Italy* (Princeton: Princeton University Press, 1993), p. 130.

11. Huntington, *The Clash of Civilizations*, p. 225.

12. Ibid., p. 319.

13. See Heath B. Chamberlain, "On the Search for Civil Society in China," *Modern China* 19(2) (1993), pp. 199–215, for a similar argument about civil society in the People's Republic.

14. See Zhang Maogui, *Shehui Yundong yu Zhengzhi Zhuanhua [Social Movements and Political Change]* (Taipei: Guojia Zhengce Yanjiu Ziliao Zhongxin, 1990).

15. This is based on research conducted jointly with Hsin-Huang Michael Hsiao. See also Hsin-Huang Michael Hsiao, *Qishi Niandai Fan Wuran Zili Jiuji de Jiegou yu Guocheng Fenxi [Analysis of the Structure and Process of Anti-pollution Self-help Movements in the 1980s]* (Taipei: Xingzheng Yuan Huanjing Baohu, 1988), on the earlier period.

16. Hsin-Huang Michael Hsiao, "The Nonprofit Sector in Taiwan: Current State, New Trends and Future Prospects" (report to the Asia Pacific Philanthropy Consortium, NGO Sector Preparatory Meeting, Bangkok, 1988).

17. These factors, plus the global example of civil values elsewhere, are identified as crucial to earlier waves of democratization in Samuel H. Huntington, *The Third Wave: Democratization in the Late Twentieth Century* (Norman: University of Oklahoma Press, 1991).

18. Francis Fukuyama, "The End of History?"

19. See Max Weber, *The Religion of China: Confucianism and Taoism*, ed. and trans. Hans H. Gerth (New York: Free Press, 1951), and Robert N. Bellah, "Epilogue: Religion and Progress in Modern Asia," in Robert N. Bellah, ed., *Religion and Progress in Modern Asia* (New York: Free Press, 1965), pp. 168–229, on religion. See Marion J. Levy, *The Family Revolution in Modern China* (Cambridge, Mass.: Harvard University Press, 1949), pp. 354–359, on the family.

20. There are, of course, alternatives to modernization theory. One of the most important has been world systems theory, which pointed out that all developing nations modernize in a world altered by the original growth of market-dominated economies in Europe—there was only a single world case of capitalism, and that limited the possibilities open to the rest of the world. Wallerstein has recently expanded this analysis to include culture, arguing that a contradictory but mutually necessary pair of ideas—racism/sexism and universalism—spreads along with the system and helps to paper over its inherent contradictions. See Im-

manuel Wallerstein, "Culture as the Ideological Battleground of the Modern World-System," *Theory, Culture & Society* 7 (1990), pp. 31–55. Typically for this kind of analysis, however, culture appears as both just a functionalist prop for the economic system and a reflex of the core toward which the periphery has no significant input.

21. Max Weber, *The Protestant Ethic and the Spirit of Capitalism*, trans. Talcott Parsons (New York: Scribner's, 1958), p. 104.

22. Karl Polanyi's *The Great Transformation* (Boston: Beacon Press, 1957) focused a great deal of attention on the cultural costs of modernity. Important later works followed through on the point, like Eric Wolf's discussion of the weakening of multistranded social ties, *Peasants* (Englewood Cliffs, N.J.: Prentice-Hall, 1966).

23. E. P. Thompson, "The Moral Economy of the English Crowd in the Eighteenth Century," *Past and Present* 50 (1971), pp. 76–136.

24. James C. Scott, *Weapons of the Weak: Everyday Forms of Peasant Resistance* (New Haven: Yale University Press, 1985).

25. Michael T. Taussig, *The Devil and Commodity Fetishism in South America* (Chapel Hill, N.C.: University of North Carolina Press, 1980).

26. See for example, Mark Granovetter, "Economic Action and Social Structure: The Problem of Embeddedness," *American Journal of Sociology* 91(3) (1985), pp. 481–510.

27. Huang Chün-chieh and Wu Kuang-ming, "Taiwan and the Confucian Aspiration: Toward the Twenty-first Century," in Stevan Harrell and Huang Chün-chieh, eds., *Cultural Change in Postwar Taiwan* (Boulder: Westview Press, 1994), p. 82.

28. Ibid., p. 83.

29. Tensions with the perceived loss of community values through the market are complicated by the historical origins of capitalism in the West, and its concomitant ties to colonialism and economic power. Antimarket and anti-Western movements may easily blur.

30. Chinese repression of most indigenous pietistic religious groups throughout the late imperial period and continuing in the People's Republic (and Taiwan until recently) was for similar reasons. Most of these groups, most of the time, had absolutely no political ambitions, but the state recognized a threat in their potential to mobilize people beyond its vision and control. See Robert P. Weller, "Ideology, Organization and Rebellion in Chinese Sectarian Religion," in Janos M. Bak and Gerhard Benecke, eds., *Religion and Rural Revolt* (Manchester: Manchester University Press, 1984), pp. 390–406.

31. See, for example: Granovetter, "Economic Action and Social Structure"; Putnam, *Making Democracy Work*; Robert D. Putnam, "Bowling Alone: America's Declining Social Capital," *Journal of Democracy* 6(1) (1995), pp. 65–78. Francis Fukuyama's *Trust* makes use of a similar framework.

32. These include Granovetter, "Economic Action and Social Structure," and Fukuyama, *Trust*. On China, see Stevan Harrell, "Why Do the Chinese Work So Hard?," *Modern China* 11(2) (1985), pp. 203–226; S. Gordon Redding, *The Spirit of Chinese Capitalism* (Berlin: Walter de Gruyter, 1990); and Yu Yingshi, *Zhongguo Jinshi Zongjiao Lunli yu Shangren Jingshen [Modern Chinese Religious Ethics and Business Spirit]* (Taipei: Lunjing, 1987).

33. See especially Putnam, *Making Democracy Work*, and Fukuyama, *Trust*. For a more general discussion of trust in civil society, see Adam Seligman, *The Idea of Civil Society* (New York: Free Press, 1992).

34. Putnam, "Bowling Alone," p. 77.

35. Alexis de Tocqueville, *Democracy in America*, rev. ed., vol. 1, ed. Francis Bowen and Phillips Bradley (New York: Vintage, 1954 [1945]).

36. Michal Buchowski, "The Shifting Meanings of Civil and Civic Society in Poland," in Chris Hann and Elizabeth Dunn, eds., *Civil Society: Challenging Western Notions* (London: Routledge, 1996), p. 84.

37. See Zhang, *Shehui Yundong yu Zhengzhi Zhuanhua*.

38. See Seligman, *The Idea of Civil Society*, for an excellent summary. Seligman expresses doubts about the utility of the concept even for the West after the changes of the last several centuries. From another point of view, Chris Hann ("Introduction: Political Society and Civil Anthropology," in Hann and Dunn, eds., *Civil Society*, pp. 1–26), argues that the idea is too closely bound to the West to provide much analytic help elsewhere.

39. See Robert W. Hefner, "From Civil Society to Democratic Civility," in Robert W. Hefner, ed., *Democratic Civility: The History and Cross-cultural Possibility of a Modern Ideal* (New Brunswick, N.J.: Transaction, 1998).

40. Ibid.

41. Seligman, *The Idea of Civil Society*.

42. See, for example, the essays in Hann and Dunn, eds., *Civil Society*. Hann's introduction is especially relevant. For specific examples, see Jenny B. White, "Civic Culture and Islam in Urban Turkey," in Hann and Dunn, eds., *Civil Society*, pp. 143–154, on Turkey; or Robert W. Hefner, "A Muslim Civil Society? Indonesian Reflections on the Conditions of Its Possibility," in Hefner, ed., *Democratic Civility*, on Indonesia.

43. I take the term "democratic civility" from Robert W. Hefner, "From Civil Society to Democratic Civility."

44. See G. Waylen, "Women and Democratization: Conceptualizing Gender Relations in Transition Politics," *World Politics* 46 (1994), pp. 327–354, on the importance of gender in democratization.

45. The major work opening up this line of analysis was Margery Wolf's *Women and the Family in Rural Taiwan* (Stanford: Stanford University Press, 1972).

46. For instance, Fukuyama (*Trust*, p. 75) claims that "the lack of trust outside the family makes it hard for unrelated people to form groups or organizations, including economic enterprises. In sharp contrast to Japan, Chinese society is *not* group oriented." The underlying image here is Marx's Asiatic mode of production where the state directly controls family groups who are otherwise unorganized.

2

Legacies

This chapter explores associational life in late imperial times, with an eye on the kinds of legacies these associations left for modern political change. A great deal of controversy over exactly this issue has erupted recently, inspired by the revival of interest in civil society in Eastern Europe. Some argue that there was an increasingly active public sphere by the last century of imperial rule in China, and others reply sharply that whatever existed was far from a civil society.[1] This chapter draws on their data, but moves outside the misleading concentration of this debate on civil society in the European sense. A more fruitful question is what kinds of social capital existed in late imperial China, and what kinds of possibilities did it create for political change.

In contrast to the pessimistic "totalitarian political culture" view of China, I will show that there were many kinds of horizontal ties that connected people into associations between family and state. The wide range of these horizontal institutions shows the great cultural diversity that formed a pool of potential change in China. Whatever Confucian bureaucrats may have hoped for, there was no single political culture. This range of variation created many options for China's future, just as a wide range of genetic variation allows a species to adapt to new conditions, while a genetically uniform population cannot survive outside its original niche.

Philosophical Legacies and Key Terms

The neo-Confucian ideology that dominated Chinese politics for much of the last millennium left no room to distinguish state from society, except in the way that fathers can be distinguished from sons. These ideas developed as a kind of Confucian philosophical rearmament in the eleventh and twelfth centuries, after a long period of official interest in competing philosophical systems, including Buddhism and Daoism. Like any Confucians, these philosophers built a moral and political universe around Confucius's original discussion of the five fundamental social relationships, each with its appropriate attitude: righteous loyalty between ruler and minister, affectionate responsibility between father and son, attention to proper roles between husband and wife, proper hierarchy between elder and younger brother, and faithfulness between friends. Family and politics are intertwined here, and the relations of ruler/minister and father/son are explicitly compared to each other. Rulers, for example, should treat the common people as their children. When Confucius, in *The Doctrine of the Mean*, goes on to explain how to apply these relationships, he offers nine standards by which to administer both the state and the family.[2] Indeed, family and state are fundamentally part of the same set of relationships, and there simply is no space between them. Ruler or father or local elite led (in principle) by upright example, by maintaining proper relations of hierarchy. As a rhetorical strategy, the equation between family and state often appears as a justification for totalizing attempts at social control—Salazar's corporatist rule in Portugal was fond of the metaphor, and so was Mussolini's in Italy.

Yet this kind of quick summary generalizes too far. Most characterizations of Confucianism ignore, for example, Confucius's fifth relationship, the tie between friends (*you*). Of the five this is the only one between equals, and the only one that relies on neither politics nor kinship. Friendship ties were often cemented as fictive kinship. Friends used kinship terms for each other, as did students of the same teacher. These borrowed kinship terms retain the hierarchy of older and younger, but they clearly also extend social ties beyond the literal family. Fictive kinship is a fiction, a metaphor, and no one confused it with real kin ties. Friendship also had popular cultural supports in China. The most influential was the famous Peach Blossom oath that united the protagonists in the vernacular novel *Romance of the Three Kingdoms*. This oath became a model for sworn brotherhoods throughout China.

There was no agreement on the total interpenetration of the state and family life even within the realm of neo-Confucian political thought. Two of the most important political philosophers of the eleventh century, when neo-Confucianism was in its formative stages, differed precisely over how much distance should be maintained between state and society. As Peter Bol describes the argument, the reformer Wang Anshi "imagined a state without a distinction between government and society, between the political and the moral, and whose institutions fulfilled the common desires and needs of all men." Sima Guang criticized this as a danger to both economy and state, and argued instead that the state should have enough power to maintain itself, while leaving private interests to pursue their own aims.[3] While Wang's thought dominated for the next century or so, the argument remained vital, and Sima's vision of China may ultimately have been closer to what developed.[4] There are roots in Wang Anshi's ideas for modern claims of Chinese authoritarian culture, but the argument reminds us that promotion of the totalizing state was never the only voice in China, even among the political and intellectual elite.

Merit and Responsibility

Max Weber's volumes on the world religions were in part dedicated to showing why industrial capitalism developed in Europe, and not in other places that seemed to have comparable social and economic resources. In the case of China he pointed to a lack of this-worldly rationalization, which had been provided by Protestant asceticism in Europe. This carried with it an absence of the struggle of the individual against the world, even the lack of individualism as a value, that was so important in Weber's version of capitalism, and that is central to most definitions of civil society. This image of China as a mass of particularistic groupings has continued to influence social analysts up to the present.

Confucianism clearly did not authorize any kind of radical individualism, and placed individuals firmly in a web of social ties. Nevertheless, a firm sense of self was central to the philosophy. "Confucian ethics, instead of being primarily a social or group ethic, as it is often referred to, starts with self-cultivation, and works outward from a proper sense of self to the acceptance of reciprocal responsibilities with others in widening circles of personal relationship concentric with that self."[5] Neo-Confucians were expected to reform themselves (*ge shen*) first, and to remain faithful to that sense of self-worth while meeting social responsibilities. Most scholars hoped to serve the state, but never blindly. Scholars who dared to criticize an arrogant and erroneous state have been honored at least since Qu Yuan drowned himself in protest over two thousand years ago. Education was a key to this transformation of self, and while it began as rote memorization, it ended as a dialog with one's teachers and with the classics. This fostered a genuine intellectual search, as well as close ties between students and teachers, and among fellow students of the same teacher.

There was thus a kind of Confucian "inner-worldly asceticism" that was not so inconsistent with Weber's characterization of Protestantism.[6] This is not to argue that Confucian China was on the verge of following in Western footsteps (as some have argued about capitalism). Many other features of the imperial heritage prevented that. Yet here was a cultural resource available in Confucianism itself that could become relevant later on. There were also other kinds of individualism available outside Confucianism. Buddhists in particular were often criticized for being overly concerned with individuals instead of the state. Some forms of popular Buddhism particularly elaborated the individual consequences of karma. By the late Ming Dynasty, popular morality books (*shanshu*) instructed people how to keep track of their individual moral merits and demerits.[7] Daoism's rejection of the state and celebration of eccentric individuals, especially in its quirky immortals (*xian*), is an even more obvious example.

Key Terms

One way to explore the various cultural streams relevant to voluntary associations and the relations between state and society is through some of the key Chinese terms that address these issues. An obvious starting point is *li*, which is usually translated as politeness (perhaps "civility" would be better in this context) or ritual behavior. Both civility and ritual are ways of giving external expression to the proper order of relationships in the universe. In contrast to some modern views, ritual and politeness were not mere formalities at best, and hypocrisies at worst. When the emperor undertook the symbolic first plowing, or when he wore black and worshipped in the north in the winter, he was in fact keeping the universe in its proper order. When he spoke to his ministers or received tributary missions in a certain way, he did the same thing. The situation was no different when a father acted with benevolence toward a son, or a man acted with faith toward his friend. In principle the proper ordering of the universe was kept up by every act of mundane courtesy in just the same way as every major ritual did.

The importance of *li* is clear from its institutionalized role in the state. The imperial government typically had six main ministries, called the Six Boards. These included things like revenue and punishment, as one might expect. They also invariably included a Board of Rites (Li Bu), which was responsible for being sure that *li* was properly carried out, at least as far as the government could control it. They oversaw the execution of the annual cycle of imperial and official rituals, and also organized the reception of tribute from foreign lands. They even ran the civil service examinations, which tested knowledge of *li* as the proper relationships within society and between humanity and the broader universe.

Part of the neo-Confucian revival was a systematic attempt to invigorate *li* by reforming ritual beyond the state. Several of the greatest minds of the period wrote instruction manuals for the performance of family rituals like weddings and funerals. Sima Guang, whom I have already mentioned, wrote one that began with a discussion of how to write civil letters properly and finished with family rituals. Zhu Xi, who wrote in the twelfth century and became the most influential figure in the movement, also authored a book of family rituals, the descendants of which are still available in bookstores.[8]

While *li* is very much about civility, its cosmological implications go far beyond the idea of civilized refinement. Its relation to European civility is thus mixed. Both concepts imply acceptance of a mutual set of understandings that allow peaceful social interaction to continue even when people disagree. This is crucial to any kind of democratic civility. On the other hand, such action in China was part of a far greater cosmos, and so formed a continuum with greater rituals like ancestor worship, weddings, or imperial invocations of the seasons. This cosmos was ultimately united in the Way, of which *li* is the outer expression. As I will discuss in Chapter 3 on authoritarianism, *li* as civility continued to be an important value in China and Taiwan throughout the twentieth century. It was promoted by every variety of state in that time, and rarely to the benefit of a democratic civility. Civility may be a necessary precondition for democracy, but it is by no means sufficient. It has more frequently been a prop of authoritarian rule, and certainly fit very easily with the imperial Chinese state as well.

Another relevant term is *gong*, which means "public," specifically in contrast to the realm of the "private" (*si*) at one end and the "official" (*guan*) at the other. By the Qing Dynasty this term usually indicated local institutions serving community functions and run by members of the elite (although the roots of such institutions go much earlier). These included things like educational academies, emergency relief granaries, self-defense militias, or religious charities. None of them were direct creations of the bureaucracy. As the imperial state faltered in the nineteenth century, these organizations and the local elites that supported them took on increasingly important and independent roles.[9]

The term *gong* could refer to anything in the public interest, including actions of the state. It contrasted especially with "private" interests, which were condemned as personalistic ties that ran counter to the state-society. When *gong* was contrasted with officialdom, it still had implications that the elite were acting on behalf of the state, whose values and goals they shared even if they were not (yet) part of the world of officials. Given the lack of a strong distinction between state and society, *gong* could not have the same implications that "public" did in Europe. These were local elites acting in consort with the state/society, and generally not promoting their own interests to (or against) the state. As with *li*, the "public" sphere in late imperial China would have to enter a completely different kind of relationship to the state before it could become relevant to anything comparable to civil society in Europe.[10]

The final indigenous term I will discuss is *wen*, which literally means writing. More broadly it refers to the kind of cultured civilization to which elites aspired and that marked the clearest difference between China and the less lettered world beyond the Great Wall and over the sea. It is used, for instance, in the terms *wenming* (civilized, literally lettered and bright), *wenhua* (culture or to enculturate), and *wenya* (elegant). "Civilization" has evolved into a particularly important term in this context. The People's Republic has strongly promoted "civilized" behavior, and "civilized society" is the translation of "civil society" most often seen there. As "culture" it is more akin to earlier Western uses (some people have culture and others do not) than the modern anthropological understanding of the term. In colloquial Chinese in the People's Republic, cultural level is synonymous with educational achievement. *Wen* also refers to civil authorities, as opposed to the military (*wu*).

China expressed its own self-image through such terms, seeing culture or civilization defined in part as Chinese literacy, and thus as a clear marker between classes of people and between China and other nations. The various combinations of *wen* thus overlap interestingly with various civil-based words in English—civilized, civil authority, civility, civilian. Yet the ties to literacy, class, and specifically Chinese identity leave it rather different from "civil society."[11]

Even today Chinese has no agreed-upon term to translate the Western idea of civil society, in contrast to the many other bits of social science jargon it borrowed in the early twentieth century from Japan, which borrowed in turn directly from Europe. Instead there is a host of neologisms including *wenming shehui* (civilized society), *gongmin shehui* (society of citizens), *shimin shehui* (bourgeois, in the sense of urban, society), or *minjian shehui* (popular society). All of these terms occur in both the People's Republic and Taiwan, but with rather different implications. It is ironic but not accidental that the socialist People's Republic favors the elitist "civilized society" whereas newly democratic Taiwan favors "popular society." None of them easily capture the connotations of the English term, and for good reason—"civil society" was, until the twentieth century, a very exotic concept for nearly all Chinese.

None of the indigenous concepts assume the separate interests of state and society. *Li*, as ritual/social propriety, implied a harmonious reverberation of microcosm and macrocosm, between the hierarchies of mutual responsibility from within the family to the emperor himself, and within the system of ritual behavior that emanated from the emperor down to the householder. *Gong* indeed meant public, but more in the sense of "public interest" than a Habermasian "public sphere." Local elites, even when they acted on their own, would have had great difficulty thinking of themselves as anything other than an aspect of an overarching sociopolitical unity, except in times of great political weakness. It is no accident that elite horizontal institutions like academies or charities thrived during periods like the southern Song or late Ming, when politics was at its most chaotic.[12] Yet none of this forces us to dismiss the possibility that these concepts could become useful in a future democratic civility. They offer a cultural framework for civil behavior, for social institutions beyond the family, and for elite self-organization of activities in the public interest.

Institutional Legacies

The Chinese idea of the state-society as an organic whole left room for argument within Confucian philosophy about how interfering the state should be. Yet the general view of the world was very different from the Enlightenment backdrop to the original civil society idea. China entered the twentieth century with a very different legacy from Europe. On the other hand, given the extraordinary political shocks and transformations that have shaken China since the nineteenth century, these ideas contain the possibility of change once unmoored from the imperial system. When we turn from elite ideas to actual social relationships it is even easier to see how indigenous social capital could form the armature for new forms of democratic civility.

Local Elites

Whatever Confucian philosophers may have wished, China was filled with networks of horizontal ties that extended beyond the immediate family but were not themselves political. China had many kinds of such resources, in spite of the lack of a *political* culture of civil society. Elites often united locally around philanthropic institutions like relief granaries or temples, especially during periods when the central government was weak and local ties became even more important. Such responsibilities belonged in principal to the primary organs of the state/society—the government and the family. In practice, however, there were large gaps that local elites filled on behalf of the greater good. The imperial state had in fact long sponsored public granaries and other welfare activities, and lineages had looked after their members since the Song Dynasty. Yet many needs remained, and a major self-organization of the local elite began in the late Ming Dynasty (sixteenth century). Their new associations included popular groups to promote Buddhist values (especially to save the lives of animals, *fangsheng hui*), and the subsequent popularity of private philanthropic groups run by local elites and dedicated to helping the local poor.[13]

This late Ming rise of "gentry society" was the beginning of a partially autonomous sphere of action for local elites departing from the Ming state's view of its own patriarchal authority.[14] In part, a newly commercialized economy (related to the influx of Spanish silver at the time) made this possible both by creating elite interests independent from the state, and by building up enough wealth to carry out such activities. For them, "Buddhism mapped an alternative world, not just of belief, but of action: a world of associational undertakings through which elite status could be cast in high-cultural terms that did not rely on definitions handed down by the state."[15] Community-based philanthropy let local Confucian elites and merchants join together in a cause that justified the new cash as an answer to social problems. Charity, after all, is a fundamentally nonmarket way of redistributing wealth. This strategy also created a popularizing tendency in the groups, as merchants increasingly influenced association policies.

Local elites also found more informal occasions to strengthen their social networks of patronage and friendship. The late Ming, for example, brought an intensification of garden culture and book appreciation. Both fads allowed wealthy elites to invest in a kind of conspicuous consumption that also proclaimed their taste and sophistication. Gardens particularly showed the ability of the owner to perceive, reproduce, and control the Way of nature. Above all, both books and gardens provided opportunities to interact with peers. They proclaimed the kind of person the owner was while they cemented social networks. They also provided an opportunity for the local elite, or at least factions of it, to cement informal solidarities.[16] Temple plazas and teahouses often served the same function for ordinary commoners, much like the European coffeehouses that Habermas celebrates.

Local and sometimes national communities could also be invoked through all kinds of *tong* ("same") ties—*tong xiang* (same native place), *tong xue* (same study, usually having had the same teacher or having passed the exams in the same year), *tong xing* (same surname, usually with no traceable kinship), and so on. Such ties created potential networks across China and beyond. The partners were united by bonds of trust guaranteed by the larger social communities to which they referred. Two people from the same county living in a big city might not have had any direct social ties, but both maintained multifaceted ties back to the same community, which would discourage breaches of trust. These ties were often not institutionalized, but they could be under the right circumstances. Sojourners in late imperial cities frequently organized by common native place and common surname, and these organizations grew into some of the most important urban communities by the twentieth century. Immigrants united around the same kinds of ties—both common surname associations and native place associations—are still pervasive in Chinatowns anywhere in the world. These ties continue to be important today. Surname associations are growing in cities, and classmate ties are more important than ever in creating business connections.

Village Connections

Other kinds of ties united more ordinary people at local levels. Religion and ritual in particular brought people together to worship community gods, appease wandering ghosts, celebrate marriages and mourn deaths. This kind of religion was based in temples without priests; community committees ran them and they were considered public property of the community. Large rituals explicitly marked out local territory by having the god parade over his turf, riding in a sedan chair and surrounded by the same kind of pomp as a magistrate on a tour of his county. Smaller rituals like funerals did the same by marching through village streets, with most of the villagers accompanying the coffin up to the border. Patterns of reciprocal feasting at every important ritual further brought people together. In some cases, temples were the only important organizations uniting villagers as communities.

The close ties between temples and communities made religion an important nexus of power and action. Local elites, or factions of them, controlled most important temples. They took on quasi-political responsibilities, not just in the accoutrements of imperial authority that dressed the gods and their rituals, but in the fiscal authority to collect funds and sometimes the military authority to organize local defense. In the area of Taiwan where I first worked, the local temple had organized people to fight the Japanese in 1895. In rural Guangxi in the 1840s, the major local temple housed the first militia formed to oppose the Taiping rebels.[17]

There was very little central control over temples like these, either from the government or from any higher religious authority. Even when temples worshipped deities of national significance (which was by no means always the case), their local significance tended to overwhelm other layers of meaning. The combination of the lack of centralized interpretive control over religion and its importance to local power made it an arena in which alternative interpretations often overlapped and sometimes collided. The imperial state regularly attempted to impose its own interpretations, for example by granting a title to a deity and inscribing its own version of the story on stone in front of the temple. These attempts often added a layer of meaning, but rarely succeeded in displacing more local layers. A number of studies show us these processes in action, for example when the spirit of a dead girl began by helping local fishermen in distress (and so came to be worshipped as Mazu) and ended with the glorious title of Empress of Heaven (Tian Hou), bestowed by the emperor. Her increasing incorporation and adulation by the state, however, did not end alternative interpretations. As James Watson shows, she conveyed the idea of pacification of imperial enemies (particularly "Japanese" pirates) to officials who promoted her cult, but she meant independence to Taiwanese (who never accepted the imperial title of Empress of Heaven), local coastal pacification to large lineage elites in the Canton delta, fertility to their wives, and so on.[18] In every case that has been looked at, popular religion is strikingly local, both in its social organization and its interpretations. It is without doubt an important organization between family and state. Yet it is also localist and communal in orientation, making it only an awkward fit at best with civil society (as I discuss further in chapter 5).

Lineages similarly could be major actors at the local level, but rarely achieved a broader stage unless they had produced an extraordinary number of degree holders. The many villages in China named after their dominant surname group testifies to the importance of lineage through much of the country, although they only developed into corporate land-holding groups in some areas.[19] In many cases, however, they offered mutual aid and a structure for village interaction. Like village and town temples, lineages had a fundamentally local focus, and could occasionally come into conflict with authorities.

Lineages are the most particularistic of ties—kinship—writ large. But writing kinship large is itself an important transformation. When lineages brought together thousands of people, as they sometimes did, they formed a kind of tie that went far beyond family, even though it remained rooted in kinship. Lineages are more than just gigantic families, but they are also fundamentally local in their interests and essentially communal in their membership. These are exactly the areas in which popular religious organizations also look very different from classical civil society. Lineages and local temples are both examples of local shareholding corporations, which were extremely common in late imperial China.[20] All of these associations shared an institutional and legal existence that placed them squarely between family and state, even as they drew on relatively communal and local kinds of ties.

Some organizations, however, partially overcame both the localism and the communalism. Emigrant communities abroad and urban sojourners within China, for instance, quickly widened the net of lineage into common surname associations. Religion burst its local bounds in China's long tradition of secret societies and closely related popularizing Buddhist sects. Many of these organizations (based on master/disciple relations in some cases, and sworn brotherhoods in others) traveled up and down China's communication routes with the rivermen (and later railroad workers) who plied them. Such groups contained an inherent potential to rebel against the state (like the White Lotus rebellion), or to evolve into gangster organizations (as in the tongs and Triads infamous in Chinese emigrant communities). Yet they were primarily voluntary pietistic associations, membership in which implied the same kinds of trust that Weber attributed to Protestant sect membership.[21]

Rotating credit associations were (and are) another common tie that could cut across local divisions of family and lineage. These were small groups of men or women who made monthly contributions to a common pot, generally taken by the highest bidder each month. Much as in other parts of the world where they are equally common, such organizations in essence provide loans at interest for people who have no other sources of credit beyond usurious moneylenders. More important in this context, they provide a kind of map of networks of community trust. Such associations always left open the possibility that someone would take the money and leave town without making the rest of their payments. Rotating credit associations thus could not function without high levels of horizontal trust.

Where Are the Women?

Women have been conspicuously absent from this discussion, largely because women were kept away from the formal, institutional arenas that are best known. Women, for example, did not take part in major lineage rituals, even though they conducted the bulk of the daily domestic worship of their husbands' ancestors. They did not organize large temple rituals, and were barred from entering temples during the most important rituals. They were not members of share-holding corporations, and did not serve on temple committees. In addition to the clear hierarchy between husband and wife in the Confucian five relationships, Confucius also summed up women's proper roles in life as the "three obediences"— to her father, then to her husband, and finally to her son. Until recent decades men referred to their wives as *neiren*, "inside people," because all their proper roles kept them inside the domestic sphere. The role of bound feet in this hardly needs mention.

Yet this concentration on formally organized institutions is misleading. Women in China appear to have taken on broader economic roles during the commercial expansion of the sixteenth century, and some male scholars at the time advocated accepting women as students.[22] Productive labor at home was important for women throughout the Qing Dynasty, even for elite women.[23] By the nineteenth century, women increasingly worked outside the home, especially in the newly industrializing textile trade. This helped create networks among women who would not ordinarily have had much contact with each other. In some cases it gave them the economic resources to drop out of patriarchal family life completely, supporting themselves in Buddhist "spinsters' houses" and sometimes buying concubines to fulfill their filial duty of bearing sons for their husbands.[24]

Elite families during the late imperial period increased their prestige by secluding their women. Even these women, however, regularly got out of the house, often in the company of other women. Visits to temples or religious masters provided one of the most important opportunities for such outings. Women got together, for example, to recite Buddhist sutras. Sutra singing groups remain an important form of horizontal connection among women today, by no means limited to elites. Women also made pilgrimages to important temples, sometimes traveling significant distances in organized groups. Susan Naquin estimates that about 10 percent of the members of formal associations to arrange pilgrimages to the temple of a goddess near Beijing in the late Qing Dynasty were women. Clearly women did this frequently enough to have spawned a large official literature worrying about the resulting deterioration of public morals.[25]

Poetry clubs probably formed the most important avenue for elite women to get together. Many thousands of women's poems survive from the late Ming and Qing Dynasties, many of which were distributed publicly through the booming publishing industry of the time. Groups of elite women formed networks of friendship, often based around a shared interest in poetry. Dorothy Ko traces the "genealogies" of several of these groups, showing how they included matrilineal kin, affines, neighbors, people from the same native place, and just friends.[26]

Outside elite groups informal ties among women were even more important. These women also visited temples and sometimes met to worship together. Perhaps more importantly, they also got together in the course of daily chores, especially to do the washing at the banks of a nearby stream. Margery Wolf was the first to show how groups of village women could exert real power through these networks, although it was a kind of informal power not recognized in a more official version of how Confucian authority worked.[27] The primary organizing principles here were gender and neighborhood. Even in the late 1970s I knew Taiwanese women with automatic washing machines who still insisted on going to the stream to clean clothes. They did not want to give up the informal community recreated each day outside the house. Village women also got together more formally at occasions like weddings. Such groups tend to remain almost invisible in the background, but could effectively apply public pressure (through their husbands) and were sometimes actively mobilized (as on occasion during the Revolution).

At least by the twentieth century, women's connections of trust had also become very important in raising capital through rotating credit associations. In Taiwan now, women may in fact be more important sources of such informal capital than men. This stems in part from men's better access to formal sources of credit like banks, but also suggests that women's networks of trust may be more reliable than men's, since the potential for breach of trust is the main weakness in this form of credit. Women's horizontal networks were generally smaller in geographic scope than men's, and they rarely burst into the formal arena. Yet they could be intimate, long-lasting, and significant for both economic and social organization.

Conclusion

This quick overview of late imperial China shows the great extent to which horizontal ties of trust permeated the society. The common caricature that "there is a very strong inclination on the part of Chinese to trust only people related to them, and conversely to distrust people outside their family and kinship group . . . [which] makes it hard for unrelated people to form groups" is a misleading oversimplification.[28] People unrelated by kinship were still linked through friendship, community membership, educational experience, charitable organizations, and religion. Even lineages are more of a social construction in China than an automatic extension of kinship. These ties were mobilized through a variety of social mechanisms, from informal gatherings around a Chinese chess game in a temple plaza to formal share-holding corporations.[29]

These ties were nearly always based in particular localities and corporate identities of various kinds—never the autonomous individuals of an idealized West. Yet it is wrong to dismiss these things as hopelessly particularistic. This was the mistake, after all, of the literature that saw little hope for economic development in Chinese societies because of the overwhelming strength of family and local loyalties. It is being repeated in some of the claims about the impossibility of democracy in Chinese nations. While this range of ties certainly did not constitute a civil society of people united in their interests as citizens, neither was it just a collection of isolated and self-serving families, united only through ties of patron and client. Various forms of extrafamilial trust existed in Chinese society, and have remained as an undeveloped possibility through all kinds of regimes. China was not behind the West on an evolutionary path toward civil society; it was its own world, to be taken on its own terms.

The Confucian placing of the family at the heart of a combined social and political morality also highlights the position of women in ways that Enlightenment and modern versions of civil society (which typically seem to contain only men) do not capture. Writing about the eighteenth century, Susan Mann makes this point through the work of the philosopher Zhang Xuechang, who

> acknowledged the dependence of public man on cloistered woman by noting that her words, too, could be "everyone's" (*gong* [public]). Based on a long history of moral philosophy placing women and the family at the center of political order, Zhang's understanding of women's public voice erases the line dividing public and private that Western political philosophy has canonized. In short, the historical record of Chinese women—both their placement in it and their consciousness as recorded there—shows a pervasive awareness of the intimate relationship between family life and public politics.[30]

Women too had their networks of trust and friendship. The scale was typically smaller than male ties, and the organizations generally less formalized. Yet they also became crucially important in the transformations of the twentieth century, as I will discuss.

Civil society and its related concepts entered China powerfully with the onslaught of Western cultural and economic globalization in the nineteenth century. The term "civil society" itself was not particularly important at first (which explains the current lack of an agreed-upon translation) in China. By the time "science" and "democracy" became watchwords of the May Fourth Movement of 1919, however, an imported political philosophy based on the separation (sometimes antagonistic) between state and society, and on the rights of autonomous individuals had become an inevitable part of all thought about China's political future. This did not, of course, lead to actual democratization, but it did begin a long conversation about the relationship of society to state that continues today.

Notes

1. A symposium in *Modern China* on "Public Sphere"/"Civil Society" in China provided a focus for the debate. See, for example, William T. Rowe, "The Problem of 'Civil Society' in Late Imperial China," *Modern China* 19(2) (1993), pp. 139–157; and Frederic Wakeman, "The Civil Society and Public Sphere Debate: Western Reflections on Chinese Political Culture," *Modern China* 19(2) (1993), pp. 108–138.

2. See, for example, the passage translated in Wing-tsit Chan, *A Source Book in Chinese Philosophy* (Princeton: Princeton University Press, 1963), pp. 105–106.

3. Peter K. Bol, "Government, Society, and State: On the Political Visions of Ssu-ma Kuang and Wang An-shih," in Robert P. Hymes and Conrad Schirokauer, eds., *Ordering the World: Approaches to State and Society in Sung Dynasty China* (Berkeley: University of California Press, 1993), p. 184.

4. Ibid., pp. 186–187.

5. William Theodore de Bary, "Confucian Education in Premodern East Asia," in Wei-ming Tu, ed., *Confucian Traditions,* p. 33.

6. See Chang Hao, "The Intellectual Heritage of the Confucian Ideal of *Ching-shih,*" in Wei-ming Tu, ed., *Confucian Traditions*, pp. 72–91. Thomas A. Metzger has long made a similar argument, for instance in his *Escape from Predicament: Neo-Confucianism and China's Evolving Political Culture* (New York: Columbia University Press, 1977).

7. See Judith A. Berling, "Religion and Popular Culture: The Management of Moral Capital in *The Romance of the Three Teachings,*" in David Johnson, Andrew J. Nathan, and Evelyn S. Rawski, eds., *Popular Culture in Late Imperial China* (Berkeley: University of California Press, 1985), pp. 188–218.

8. For a discussion of the manuals see Patricia Buckley Ebrey, *Confucianism and Family Rituals in Imperial China: A Social History of Writing About Rites* (Princeton: Princeton University Press, 1991). She has also translated and annotated the Zhu Xi manual as *Chu Hsi's Family Rituals: A Twelfth-century Chinese Manual for the Performance of Cappings, Weddings, Funerals, and Ancestral Rites* (Princeton: Princeton University Press, 1991).

9. For more on this see Mary Backus Rankin, "Some Observations on a Chinese Public Sphere," *Modern China* 19(2) (1993), pp. 158–182; and Rowe, "The Problem of 'Civil Society' in Late Imperial China."

10. The interpretation of these kinds of elite institutions in the Qing Dynasty was a key area of disagreement in a special issue of *Modern China* devoted to civil society issues in 1993. My argument here is closest to the position of Frederic Wakeman's in "The Civil Society and Public Sphere Debate."

11. Edward Shils ("Reflections on Civil Society and Civility in the Chinese Intellectual Tradition," in Wei-ming Tu, ed., *Confucian Traditions*, pp. 38–71) also emphasizes the role of civility in China, and points out that it was incorporated by the state in ways unlike its role in Western writing about civil society.

12. On the increase in such associations during the Southern Song, see Robert Hymes, *Way and Byway* (unpublished manuscript, 1996); on the late Ming, see Timothy Brook, *Praying for Power: Buddhism and the Formation of Gentry Society in Late-Ming China* (Cambridge, Mass.: Harvard-Yenching Institute, 1993). Brook also carries this argument into the twentieth century in his "Auto-Organization in Chinese Society," in Timothy Brook and Michael B. Frolic, eds., *Civil Society in China* (Armonk, N.Y.: M. E. Sharpe, 1997), pp. 19–45.

13. See Brook, *Praying for Power*, pp. 104–107 and 185–223, and Joanna F. Handlin Smith, "Benevolent Societies: The Reshaping of Charity During the Late Ming and Early Ch'ing," *Journal of Asian Studies* 46(2) (1987), pp. 309–337.

14. The term "gentry society" is from Brook, *Praying for Power*, pp. 23–29.

15. Ibid., p. 316. Joanna F. Handlin Smith emphasizes the effects of commercialization even more clearly in her "Benevolent Societies."

16. On gardens, see Joanna F. Handlin Smith, "Gardens in Ch'i Pao-chia's Social World: Wealth and Values in Late-Ming Kiangnan," *Journal of Asian Studies* 51(1) (1992), pp. 55–81; and Craig Clunas, *Fruitful Sites: Garden Culture in Ming Dynasty China*, (Durham, N.C.: Duke University Press, 1996).

17. A number of anthropological works have made these points. See, for example, P. Steven Sangren, *History and Magical Power in a Chinese Community* (Stanford: Stanford University Press, 1987), and Robert P. Weller, *Unities and Diversities in Chinese Religion* (Seattle: University of Washington Press, 1987). Historical studies of these issues are more unusual, but an excellent example is Prasenjit Duara, *Culture, Power, and the State: Rural North China, 1900–1942* (Stanford: Stanford University Press, 1988). More recently, the relevance of religion to civil society debates in China has been discussed by Paul R. Katz, *Demon Hordes and Burning Boats: The Cult of Marshal Wen in Late Imperial Chekiang* (Albany, N.Y.: State University of New York Press, 1995), pp. 180–189.

18. James L. Watson, "Standardizing the Gods: The Promotion of T'ien Hou ('Empress of Heaven') Along the South China Coast, 960–1960," in David Johnson, Andrew J. Nathan, and Evelyn S. Rawski, eds., *Popular Culture*, pp. 292–324. For other examples of this kind of thing see Weller, *Unities and Diversities*; Prasenjit Duara, "Superscribing Symbols: The Myth of Guandi, Chinese God of War," *Journal of Asian Studies* 47(4) (1988), pp. 778–795; and Brigitte Baptandier, "The Lady Linshui: How a Woman Became a Goddess," in Meir Shahar and Robert P. Weller, eds., *Unruly Gods: Divinity and Society in China* (Honolulu: University of Hawaii Press, 1996), pp. 105–149.

19. See Myron L. Cohen, "Lineage Organization in North China," *Journal of Asian Studies* 49(3) (1990), pp. 509–534.

20. See P. Steven Sangren, "Traditional Chinese Corporations: Beyond Kinship," *Journal of Asian Studies* 43(3) (1984), pp. 391–415.

21. See Weller, "Ideology, Organization, and Rebellion," and Max Weber, "The Protestant Sects and the Spirit of Capitalism," in H. H. Gerth and C. Wright Mills, eds., *From Max Weber: Essays in Sociology* (New York: Oxford University Press, 1946), pp. 302–322.

22. See Joanna F. Handlin, "Lü Kun's New Audience: The Influence of Women's Literacy on Sixteenth-century Thought," in Margery Wolf and Roxane Witke, eds., *Women in Chinese Society* (Stanford: Stanford University Press, 1975), pp. 25–26.

23. Susan Mann, *Precious Records: Women in China's Long Eighteenth Century* (Stanford: Stanford University Press, 1997), pp. 143–177.

24. See Marjorie Topley, "Marriage Resistance in Rural Kwangtung," in Wolf and Witke, eds., *Women in Chinese Society*, pp. 67–88; and Janice E. Stockard, *Daughters of the Canton Delta: Marriage Patterns and Economic Strategies in South China, 1860–1930* (Stanford: Stanford University Press, 1989). Kathy Le Mons Walker, "Economic Growth, Peasant Marginalization, and the Sexual Division of Labor in Early Twentieth-century China: Women's Work in Nantong County," *Modern China* 19(3) (1993), pp. 354–386, argues that these changes generally did not much raise women's social or domestic status. Nevertheless, they would have contributed to the creation of horizontal ties among women.

25. Susan Naquin, "The Peking Pilgrimage to Miao-feng Shan: Religious Organizations and Sacred Site," in Susan Naquin and Chün-fang Yü, eds., *Pilgrims and Sacred Sites in China* (Berkeley: University of California Press, 1992), pp. 333–377. On official feelings about women pilgrims, see also Mann, *Precious Records*, pp. 194–200.

26. Dorothy Ko, *Teachers of the Inner Chambers: Women and Culture in Seventeenth-century China* (Stanford: Stanford University Press, 1994), pp. 226–242. See also Mann, *Precious Records*, pp. 76–120.

27. Wolf, *Women and the Family in Rural Taiwan*, pp. 42–52. Nearly all the evidence we have on these dynamics is from the last century only, but without servants, non-elite women probably long shared similar responsibilities.

28. Fukuyama, *Trust*, p. 75.

29. For a similar argument, see Brook, "Auto-organization in Chinese Society."

30. Mann, *Precious Records*, p. 223.

3

The Limits to Authority

The political tumult of the twentieth century ended the political economy that had embedded the various ties of trust I have been discussing. Confucianism as a guiding political ideology died with the imperial system in 1911; the examination system and its incorporation of knowledge classes into the state project had ended a few years earlier. This is not to say that either the import of foreign political thought or the end of the earlier political system would lead to any kind of democratic civility—that was far from the case. During certain periods, however, it did open up a free space in which new kinds of horizontal institutions thrived, based on the legacies I have been discussing. Old social resources and new institutional possibilities combined, for example, in the political turmoil of 1920s Beijing:

> Old conventions guiding public behavior, like meeting in teahouses to mediate or conspire, combined with new ideologies and organizations, like unionism and political clubs and parties, to underpin a radical expansion of political participation. . . . The trembling of the state in the 1920s, the weak legitimacy of private interests (si), and the positive moral and political evaluation of gong as a zone of discussion and concern encouraged newspaper editors, new and old civic leaders, and ordinary citizens to improvise strategies and tactics for expressing political views in public.[1]

Women also found ways to mobilize in the new society. When the Chinese took over the administration of the Natural Feet Society (which opposed foot-binding) in 1906, for instance, more than 50,000 women joined in Shanghai.[2]

The room left by the late imperial state for bonds of community, religion, education, and common interest—ties of all kinds between family and state—meant that there was a significant pool of social resources that played an increasingly important role in the changes that were coming.

In the chapters that follow I will examine how these kinds of ties inter-acted with both communist and market versions of modernity as they developed into the situation of today.

The late imperial state can be seen as an attempt to impose a Confucian ideology of rule that could never fully succeed. Social life for ordinary villagers and town dwellers retained its own logic, shaped as much by the commodity economy as by the broader state. This encouraged many kinds of horizontal ties that the state accommodated but never really liked, including lineages, sworn brotherhoods, and religious sects. The state had little choice in this partly because it needed healthy local economies, and partly because it simply did not have the power to im-pose its own interpretations over its subjects. Magistrates were too far above ordinary people, and had few resources they could use to reach down into daily life.

The technologies of rule improved greatly with the new regimes of the twentieth century, while the desire for a state orthodoxy remained as strong as ever. Yet the various modernist, corporatist, and authoritarian governments that tried to reshape China over the century also failed to impose a fully successful hegemony, including the most spectacular at-tempts in the People's Republic. This chapter is about the survival of hor-izontal ties under all kinds of conditions, even in the face of powerful at-tempts to end them.

Two broad arguments might lead us to expect the demise of institu-tional life in China, one based on the general trends of modernity and the other specific to the totalitarian project. Foucault offers one of the most eloquent descriptions of the threat from modernity in his discussion of Jeremy Bentham's design for a Panopticon.[3] The Panopticon was to be an instrument for perfect surveillance and supervision of a population—prisoners, students, patients, anyone. Each individual would be sepa-rated into a separate cell, cutting them off from horizontal communica-tion and even vision. All the cells would surround and open to a central tower from which an observer could know all that occurred. This was a democratic process in the sense that the observer could be anyone; the technology of control made the mechanism possible, rather than the power of the individual at the center. Better still, because the subjects had no idea whether someone was watching them at any given time, the Panopticon could keep people under control even with no one in the tower. The idea was realized, at least to an extent, in some prisons and testing situations. It is perhaps most familiar to those of us who teach in the language laboratory, where students sit in separate carrels, subject to unpredictable eavesdropping and intervention by an invisible teacher.

For Foucault the entire enterprise is a trope for modernity, whose tech-niques of control, from census to social work, isolate us as separate individuals and subject us to the gaze of external, depersonalized power. The image leaves no room for self-organized horizontal institutions. They are impossible when walls separate us from each other. As a general process, this dissolution of society into a bureaucracy overseeing a mass of isolated individuals has been identified by all the major social thinkers who wrote about modernity. Marx saw it in his early identification of alienation as a key process of capitalism. Durkheim pointed to much the same thing in his discussion of anomie, although he felt the situation could be ameliorated without abandoning the system. The much more recent communitarian lament over an alleged decline in the horizontal institutions said to characterize American society is part of the same kind of observation.[4]

All of this is theory. Empirically, these views identify a very powerful force within modernity, but certainly not the only force. This vision of the dissolution of horizontal ties is part of the logic, after all, that led to some (false) Marxist predictions of the dissolution of the family under capitalism, and to some (also false) Weberian expectations of the inevitable secularization of organized religion. Modern societies sometimes present themselves as built around autonomous individuals, but those individuals are in fact still embedded in social ties, as I discussed in the first chapter. The case of Taiwan, which I will discuss next, shows just how important such social ties have been in their case of modernity without the complications of communism.

For communism itself theorists of totalitarianism from Hannah Arendt on have pointed even more strongly to the atomization of individuals whose only ties are to an overarching state.[5] This image differs from the Panopticon, however, in a crucial way: The identity of the observer sitting in the center is clear to everyone. That is, surveillance and control is systemic and anonymous in Foucault's vision of modernity; its institutions are spread throughout the society. Communism instead places its top leaders in a visible position of mastery. This allows for a much more unified system of control, where even the economy (again in theory only) runs at the will of the state. It also greatly changes the dynamics of resistance, because the state embodies the entire system. This creates a single target for opposition, but also empowers the forces of repression.

Yet these images of totalitarianism also describe no more than a project that is never successfully completed. As I discuss in the latter part of this chapter, communism has never fully wiped out horizontal ties, even in its most radical Chinese forms. China recognized early on, for example, that it would have to encourage families, not dissolve them..While families are too small and particularistic for most definitions of intermediate institutions, they still represent alternative sources of social capital from the state, as Pol Pot realized so brutally in Cambodia. China has also always had to live with a "second economy" beyond the socialized sector, and has even created new kinds of horizontal ties through the system of small group meetings. These were meant to supplement other forms of state control, but also created new kinds of ties of trust as an unintended but inevitable consequence. No Chinese state—imperial, authoritarian, and capitalist like most of Taiwan's history after the Japanese occupation, or communist—has successfully wiped out self-organized, horizontal institutions, although some have certainly pushed hard on them. Yet, as the comparison between Taiwan and the People's Republic in this chapter will show, the manner in which the state incorporates those groupings makes an enormous difference for their potential political consequences.

Taiwan and the Republic of China

The fall of the last dynasty in 1911 brought China an era of political disorder interspersed with the modernist authoritarian rule of Chiang Kaishek, who controlled the Republic effectively for fifty years, until his death in 1975. There was nothing civil about this society, in spite of a few trappings of democracy. The Nationalist (KMT) regime had been powerfully (if tacitly) influenced by Leninist political and military organization ever since the first United Front with the Communists (in 1924), although Chiang later also used Nazi military models. The regime is generally recognized as having been largely corrupt, brutal, and ineffective. Voices outside the central authorities were channeled through corporatist institutions at best, and crushed at worst. The warlords who ruled where Chiang did not were still worse.

"Civility"

Even at the most authoritarian times, however, "civility" and "civilization" played important roles in various ideological campaigns under Chiang and the KMT. The Communists would later revive very similar campaigns. The Nationalist version peaked under Chiang in the 1930s, with the New Life Movement, a broad campaign for personal hygiene and polite behavior. The goals sound trivial, but the stakes were high. The campaign drew in part on Western ideas of civility and citizenship—harnessing the image of a "civil" society to a not-so-civil state. It also harked back to Confucian values, including *li*, interpreted in the most authoritarian sense as externally exposed discipline. The goal, ultimately, was to extend state control by letting the state dominate the micropractices of daily life.[6] The campaign intended to remake identity in ways that would be both modern and malleable to the will of the government. A cultural ideal of civility may be necessary to a civil society, but it certainly is not sufficient.

Civility here becomes a kind of ethical cage, serving to promote obedience and stifle any antagonism toward the regime. The campaign was generally unsuccessful, in part because the KMT had little ability to carry out most of its mass campaigns, but also in part because an uncivil state is in a weak position to promote civility. Taiwan for a long time continued the tradition of the New Life Movement after the Nationalists took over in 1945.[7] When I first lived there in the 1970s, the police frequently picked up young men to give them involuntary haircuts, and dancing parties were illegal. Still more campaigns urged people to line up for busses and to stop spitting in public. None of this seemed to make much difference, but the campaigns went on.

Singapore's infamous ban on chewing gum is part of the same authoritarian effort at control through civility, although it does not grow from the same roots in the New Life Movement. All these campaigns promote a patronizing civility, hoping to mold an internal loyalty to the state by enforcing the outward behaviors of a well-disciplined child. The most significant difference in Singapore is that its microscopic scale has allowed it some success in these campaigns; the streets really are clean there. In each case "civility" has been borrowed to promote a docile populace and not to guarantee an independent one, to enhance the scope of the state and not to support a distinct civil society. Not all civility is democratic civility. State control over the micropractices of social interaction, the enforcement of official "civility," is quite different from the pluralist civility that can grow up to allow a modus vivendi for competing horizontal groups under a state that gives them free space to develop.

Corporatism

Political scientists often refer to Taiwan's system up to the democratic reforms of the late 1980s as corporatist, where interest groups are created by the state (or at least licensed by it) as the sole representative for their sector (farmers, workers, youth, and so on). In return for their monopoly, these groups are expected to act in concert with the state. In Taiwan's authoritarian version of this system before martial law was lifted the government maintained strong control over officials of these organizations, who thus acted more as agents of the state than lobbyists for their constituents.[8] The KMT had broadly penetrated all official interest groups by the end of the 1950s, and some such organizations, like the Farmers' Association, had become central instruments for policy implementation.

By the time I lived there in the 1970s this system had long been consolidated. While local economic life was relatively unfettered, the hand of the state lay heavy indeed over other aspects of life, especially when there was any imaginable political consequence. Broadcast and print media were strictly controlled, and foreign print media were censored. Education was powerfully ideological, from its strong attacks on "Communist bandits" (*gong fei*) to the insistence that local languages could not be used in school. It was illegal to read Marx, and even unflattering pictures of Mao Zedong were kept out. There was only one significant political party. It was possible to run as a candidate with no party affiliation, but this created immediate financial and organizational inequalities in every election. If that were not enough, I also heard accusations of vote rigging if the right candidate were in danger of losing. Police kept an eye on long-term foreigners like me, and I was photographed when they learned I had an academic connection to someone in the dissident movement. Dissidents faced exile or long prison terms of hard labor.[9]

For all that, however, the authoritarian system was nowhere near complete. Although the KMT maintained a smothering grip on politics, it allowed genuinely competitive village-level elections. It also said it was dedicated to democracy; that may have been meant by some as mere lip service (certainly it seemed like it to me at the time), but even lip service can eventually shape a discourse. The local elections could not give rise to any alternative party politics, and rival candidates often both had KMT affiliations. This process encouraged a pattern of localized political factions in Taiwan. These factions are not formally institutionalized, but do have clear collective identities that have lasted for many decades in most areas.[10] They continue to be strongly influential under the current democratic system, and show the kind of powerful local network that could be constructed even in the most constrained area of life in Taiwan.

A similar combination of domineering state and lively local alternatives occurred in cultural policy.[11] The early postwar years saw a concerted effort to remove Japanese influences on Taiwanese culture, to force the island to speak Mandarin instead of local languages or Japanese, and to promote a strongly nationalist and anti-Communist agenda. Children were struck, and later fined, for speaking their native languages in school. Taiwan's government tried to champion its Confucian values, largely as a claim to be the true cultural center of China with the mainland occupied by "bandits." Journals that stepped too far from the official line—too liberal, too Western avant-garde, too Taiwanese—were shut down, and their leaders were sometimes arrested. In spite of all this, however, alternatives flourished. Taiwanese-language folk music and cinema thrived in the late 1950s, and some intellectuals showed their interest in Taiwanese folk customs as something worth studying for its own sake. Some of this activity was repressed in the decades that followed, but alternatives still managed to pop up, like the "nativist literature" (*xiangtu wenxue*) movement of the 1970s, which was a search for identity with local roots. These controls finally loosened in the 1980s, bringing a kind of cultural renaissance, but also building on things that had already developed in the cracks of the old system.

The Example of Ghosts

Popular religious practice offers numerous examples of this ability to find the free space in even a very authoritarian system. The history of ghost worship in Taiwan over the last century provides a clear case of the survival of alternate values even in the face of harsh repression. The annual ritual for the salvation of lonely ghosts (Pudu) in Taiwan continued, sometimes in disguise, against opposition from the Qing Dynasty, Japanese colonialism, and finally KMT rule.[12]

People throughout this period thought of ghosts as marginal beings, as they did across China. Ghosts are the unincorporated dead, spirits who have no descendants to worship them (and so are not ancestors), and who also have no individual identity or local cult based on their extraordinary help to the living (and so are not deities). At different times and places ghosts may be seen as pitiful souls who languish uncared for in the underworld, or as dangerous and unpredictable carriers of sickness and death. Most people make offerings to them only when they are diagnosed as causing illness, and at the annual festival of Universal Salvation in the seventh lunar month each year.

Buddhist or Daoist priests coordinate the festival, and perform rituals to feed and comfort the ghosts, and to end their suffering. At least in some parts of Taiwan, the performance in the late nineteenth century frequently turned violent. Massive crowds would gather for the culmination of the priestly rituals, when the head priest ritually transformed the massive amounts of food offerings into even more massive (but invisible) amounts that could feed all the gathered ghosts. The real food offerings were piled onto raised platforms topped with poles that rose dozens of feet into the air. Masses of unruly young toughs would fight each other trying to steal the food offerings and the flags at the tops of the poles. The offerings were thought to bring good luck, and there was a market for the flags. The event was always partially out of control, and it sometimes deteriorated into a riot, even as late as the 1920s.

An early missionary describes the crowd of "hungry beggars, tramps, blacklegs, desperadoes of all sorts." When the priests gave the signal,

> like demons of the pit . . . , in one wild scramble, groaning and yelling all the while, trampling on those who had lost their footing or were smothered by the falling cones, fighting and tearing one another like mad dogs, they all made for the coveted food. It was a very bedlam, and the wildness of the

scene was enhanced by the irregular explosion of firecrackers and the death-groan of some one worsted in the fray.[13]

As late as the 1920s a Japanese colonial description describes how the platform of offerings was filled with people, "pushing and screaming, and robbing each other. Some people were pushed down the platform. They say that with the ghosts' protection they will not be hurt, but in fact large numbers are always hurt and killed."[14]

In all likelihood these violent performances became widespread only in the nineteenth century, although there is no way to prove the assertion. Certainly brief earlier mentions of the ceremony in Taiwan and descriptions from Fujian do not describe it in these terms. I have argued elsewhere that the rioters themselves took on the role of ghosts—they were socially marginal people acting just like starving ghosts desperate for their offerings.[15] By the late nineteenth century parts of Taiwan had recreated a level of frontier violence that had not been common for a century. This was largely the result of the new camphor trade, which brought single young Chinese men deep into Taiwan's mountains for the first time. The new trade caused several kinds of social disruption: It fostered renewed battles with aborigines whose safe mountain strongholds were now being threatened; it created large numbers of unattached young men; and it encouraged them to organize a black market trade in defiance of the government monopoly on camphor. Northern Taiwan was also filled with bandits at the time, and these young men appear to have been the heart of the violent form of the Universal Salvation.

No wonder the Qing government was alarmed by the ritual. They responded in two ways, both of which were completely ineffective. First, the imperial state sponsored its own form of the ritual at official ghost altars in each administrative center. Their own ritual texts emphasized how ghosts would serve the state by reporting malfeasance. One subprefect in the nineteenth century developed his own text aimed at ending the bloody feuds between Chinese and aborigines, and among Chinese from different places of origin.[16] Here the whole population was read as ghosts to be pacified. These attempts to co-opt the idea of ghosts failed, however, in large part because ideas of Confucian propriety caused most officials to ban common people from their state rituals. The techniques of explicit ideological control would become far more powerful a century later. The second reaction was simply to make these ritual performances illegal. Again, however, the Taiwan government did not have the power to enforce its law, and the unruly ghosts of most Taiwanese were not effectively challenged.

The Japanese occupation that began in 1895 did not take an active stance toward popular religion at first. Temples destroyed in the initial resistance to the Japanese were reconstructed, although large and expensive reconstructions were not generally allowed. Yet this relative laissez-faire changed considerably during the 1930s. By this time a generation of young Taiwanese had been educated in Japanese, and the buildup to the war effort in Japan created further pressures for Japanization. This meant that the colonial government did begin to repress popular religion while encouraging Japanese alternatives. The process peaked when local governments removed the god images from popular temples in a number of towns. The finer images ended up in Japanese ethnological museums, while the rest were burned. This, the government happily announced, indicated the promotion of local gods to Heaven as Shinto deities.[17] The Japanese backed away from this policy of total repression almost immediately, but they did actively continue to promote Shinto and Japanese Buddhism (which was intended to unite their Asian empire).

In spite of all this, Taiwanese were able to continue worshipping in their own ways. People became very creative in learning how to maintain rituals that were being discouraged. For example, the annual ghost festival had lost its rootless young men by the 1920s, for both political and economic reasons. The camphor trade was moribund, and the Japanese had crushed banditry and other forms of endemic violence. Yet many areas retained the ceremony with all its furor by turning it into an "athletic competition" between village teams striving to grab the best offerings from high towers. Through a similar maneuver, offerings of fattened whole pigs at a local god's birthday celebration took on the veneer of an agricultural competition.[18] This allowed villagers to claim that force-feeding pigs to be as huge as possible was an exercise in agricultural modernization rather than a wasteful superstition, or that feeding the ghosts built strong bodies rather than causing annual riots. Creative adaptations like these enabled people to insist that they were responding to government preferences. At the same time they retained as much as possible of the festival life they valued. Carrying on with these rituals in the face of government disapproval was a kind of safe defiance, where the claim for physical or agricultural competition gave the religious practice a kind of plausible deniability.

The Nationalists who retook the island in 1945 were no more fond of unruly religion than the Qing Dynasty or the Japanese. They found festivals like the Universal Salvation unsavory because they were beyond political control, consumed a great deal of cash in ways the government considered frivolous, and simply did not fit with their modernist image of themselves. This generally appeared as campaigns for frugality that peaked each year just before the festival. These efforts did succeed in getting everyone to worship on the same day, which cut down on reciprocal feasting. Yet they apparently made no dent in the festival itself. By the

1970s these campaigns had become relatively quiet, and were simply ignored.[19]

Each of these governments that ruled Taiwan for the century before its
democratization found the ghost festival objectionable for its own reasons, and each tried to repress or limit it. Yet ultimately none of them had
much direct effect. The Qing lacked the technology of rule to carry out its
policies on religion, and neither the Japanese nor the KMT ultimately
chose to risk the popular anger that would have resulted from stopping
popular practice completely. During that century the textual and priestly
core of the ritual remained unchanged, but the popular performance was
reworked over and over as people adjusted to the space left to them.
Often this put people into quiet opposition with government policy, but
this need not necessarily be the case. When I saw the festival in 1979, just
after the United States had broken diplomatic ties with the Republic of
China on Taiwan, the Universal Salvation was conspicuously frugal so
people could contribute to the national defense. On that one occasion, apparent cooperation outweighed the usual lip service to official campaigns.

Information control and cultural propaganda were powerful in Taiwan
from the latter part of the Japanese period well into the 1980s. Even
under those circumstances, however, local rituals, sometimes wearing
superficial disguises as agricultural or athletic competitions, found ways
to remain as reservoirs of local society and culture beyond the reach of
the state. Temple rituals like this one are not explicitly political—indeed
that is one reason they were allowed to survive. Yet they also offered a set
of alternative values based in local social networks. Under the right circumstances, they can easily evolve in ways that support civil society. The
defunct Japanese-era version of the festival, for example, has recently
been revived in Ilan, once again as a competition among village athletic
teams to climb the altars and retrieve food offerings and flags. In an
ironic turn, the local government has promoted the revival in an attempt
to attract tourist trade to a Taiwanese "authenticity." The festival has
bloomed again with democracy, but even the worst of Japanese colonialism and KMT authoritarianism could not stamp it out.

The People's Republic of China

Chinese communism, especially during its most radical periods of the
Great Leap Forward and the Cultural Revolution, attempted to forge a
brand new society at all levels. In this vision the economy would gradually come to be owned communally. The process began in the most advanced industries with factories owned by the "entire people" of China
(that is, state-owned enterprises), and greatly increased with the rural

communization of land and labor in the late 1950s. Political life would also be renewed and rearranged, with factory workers sharing their entire social worlds through the unit (*danwei*) system and villages divided into brigades and teams. Constant political meetings would bring everyone actively into the polity, with no bystanders. Remnants of "feudal" culture as well as inroads from abroad would be stamped out and replaced by a new socialist identity of self-sacrifice for the greater good. No space was left in any of this for horizontal ties of trust or civil institutions independent from the state.

Visions have to face realities, however. The People's Republic developed powerful authoritarian mechanisms to carry out this vision, far exceeding all earlier Chinese states in its ability to reach into people's daily lives. Yet it also never fully succeeded, trapped partly by the legacies of the past, and partly by the very logic of the new system. This section discusses some of the primary ways in which the totalitarian project failed in China, or at least had only limited success. These limits leave a wide set of horizontal ties that remains relevant to China's future development.

Economy and Local Life

China's economy from about 1956 until the reforms of the 1980s was built around central command and control. Government experts intervened between supply and demand by determining how much of what goods would be produced, and damping or encouraging demand as they thought necessary. Prices were set to meet political and social goals. This gave the government great power to promote urban welfare, for example, by keeping housing and basic grain prices extremely low. Setting a low purchase price for crops they bought from farmers and a high price for consumer goods created funds the government could use to promote economic sectors they wanted to emphasize, usually heavy industry and its workers. Controlling prices could thus function as a particularly opaque system of indirect taxation and redistribution.

Even China's bureaucrats, however, could not manage all this down to the microscopic level. Communism was famous for its sudden lack of some item, say toothbrushes, because some official had gotten the demand wrong or sent the wrong quota to a factory. The regular shortages made standing in long lines to shop a way of life in all communist societies. People responded in part by finding alternate ways to move goods around the society. One of these was to use the remnants of the market economy. A farmer might retain a very small plot of land, for example, to grow a cash crop like tomatoes for which town dwellers hungered. The size of this second economy varied with the policy of the time, but it was generally legal throughout the history of the People's Republic. The only exception was the Great Leap Forward, when experiments with more complete communism completely disrupted the remnants of the market, and contributed to the economic disaster of the period.[20]

Another consequence of the limits to command and control was hoarding by factory managers. With no direct competition between firms, a primary goal of any manager was to control more resources from the state by requesting more and by disguising what they already had. This process also contributed to shortfalls in the economy. Perhaps more importantly, it undercut the political agenda of the center by encouraging managers to mislead the officials who were in charge of them through their statistical reporting.[21] Incentives to mislead supervisors were strong for anyone with quotas to fulfill and workers or residents to satisfy— local township officials as much as big state-owned enterprise managers.

My experience checking official statistics against data on the ground in several poor areas of China consistently showed the effects of this kind of local misreporting. In Guizhou, for example, I found that people often had more land than statistics showed, because they were farming significant tracts that were not legally registered. Local officials knew about this, but ignored it because the local people were so desperate for land. This shows up ultimately in national statistics that underestimate the amount of farmed land, and also the rates of deforestation and erosion (since much of this unregistered land is forested and steeply sloped). In other areas literacy rates or school attendance rates were systematically overestimated. Measures of public health like infant mortality rates are off because people hide births. Local officials generally know what is going on, but sometimes collude with the local people because they must continue working with them, and because they genuinely see people's welfare being served by providing false or misleading information. County officials, for example, may underestimate poverty to show the success of their administration, but may also exaggerate poverty in the hopes of getting extra aid as an officially designated poor county. All of this shows an informal side to the political economy, where local officials and managers may cooperate with locals to manipulate higher levels of the state.

The constant shortages also encouraged people to get goods by capitalizing on personal connections. This is as true of the consumer who wanted to avoid standing in line for a scarce toothbrush as of the factory manager who needed steel. Both had to rely on informal lines of communication to find out where goods were, and to gain access to those goods. Ability to pay high prices for scarce goods is not as crucial as personal connections to a range of people from shopkeepers to high officials, depending on the kinds of things needed. Scarce goods are allocated by political power, not price as in a market economy. Here again the "scientific," rationalized principles of state planning were undercut by the real logic of social life.

Many of the more ethnographic accounts of China comment on these kinds of ties. Gifts are the most important markers of this informal social sector. They reinforce existing ties, create new ones, and mark changing relationships. Some kinds of gifts are so large and so obviously self-serving that they merge into pure bribery. The great majority, however, are parts of generalized patterns of reciprocity, delineating a social network of friendship, kinship, and community, but also a network with potential economic utility. The only study so far of gift-giving budgets among peasants shows that typical families spend 20 percent of their annual income on various kinds of gifts.[22] Other studies note the same general pattern, and indeed no one who has spent significant time in China can fail to notice it.[23]

Studies of local politics show how these kinds of ties allow local leaders to manipulate the system in pursuit of benefits for their area or themselves. We have two detailed studies of brigade party secretaries, both of which show their heavy reliance on personal connections. One in Fujian explicitly explains his success as coming above all through his ability to maintain harmonious relations (*renhe*) within the village and with his old comrades who are now higher-level officials. At one point, for example, he arranges a lucrative construction contract for his villagers with the Xiamen City Traffic Control Office. There is a great deal of competition for such contracts, but he succeeds by connecting two old friends in a way that allows the Traffic Control Office to buy imported cigarettes at a low cost. He says, "I don't consider this bribery. None of us was taking graft in this deal. . . . I was merely using my connections to set up trading relationships for two parties who otherwise would not be able to deal directly."[24] A study of Chen Village in Guangdong province shows a similar pattern of manipulation of social networks, but with a heavier hand and apparently stickier fingers. The party secretary in this case drew team boundaries to help his relatives and neighbors; he effectively used his patronage to build a network and to pull more resources out of higher political levels.[25] The quick split of the early Cultural Revolution into competing local factions is also evidence for the broad extension of alternative networks in a society where everyone was supposedly tied directly and only to the central state.

Identities

These alternative kinds of social ties also foster alternative senses of self. The People's Republic has continuously campaigned for a kind of selfless

self in China, although the consistency and extent of these campaigns
have varied widely. The "people" as a unit become a kind of socialist
body, with each cell contributing in its own way to the improvement of
the whole. This message has been carried both directly and indirectly. It
has appeared indirectly, for example, in style. Clothing for most people
until the 1980s was thick blue, gray, or brown fabric cut in the style West-
erners have called "Mao suits." This may have been driven by economic
considerations—the cloth is durable, the design is practical, and the minimal variation allowed huge economies of scale in production. Yet it also
carried the message that the "people" desire utility over luxury and thrift
over consumption. By dressing everyone nearly identically, it also emphasized the lack of differentiation among the people. The generic use of
"comrade" carried the same message. When fashion loosened up in the
mid-1980s, people occasionally found themselves accused of Western or
bourgeois "spiritual pollution" for wearing the new styles.

Campaigns concerning the minutiae of individual behavior during the
1980s and 1990s have also promoted a kind of faceless equality of all, and
are disconcertingly similar to the New Life campaign of the old KMT.
The key term in these modern campaigns has been *wenming shehui*, civilized society. The rubric has included campaigns to line up, stop spitting,
and say "thank you." The general tone is of a patronizing father lecturing
an ill-mannered child. Anagnost discusses in detail how this constitutes a
state attempt to expand control over the smallest details of life, even as
government planners lose control over larger areas of the economy.[26] As
in the New Life campaign, this is done in the name of both (socialist)
modernity and Chinese tradition, in contrast to the corruption of the capitalist West.

The most explicit promotion of this selfless self has been through models for people to emulate. The revival of Cultural Revolution socialist he-
roes like Lei Feng in the last few years is another example of the attempt
to create a socialist citizen, or perhaps to read everyone as parts of the single totalitarian body.[27] Lei Feng was a young soldier who kept a detailed
diary of his love for Chairman Mao, and of the many good and generous
deeds he performed as a result. He achieved socialist beatification after
his accidental death, and was heavily promoted as a role model, especially to young students. He embodies a particular image of the selfless
self, living (and dying) for the greater good of the nation alone.

Yet these efforts too have never fully succeeded, partly because of the
nature of authoritarian control itself. Most obviously, the strong inequalities and clear hierarchies of socialist China undercut the message of
equality. Even when clothing was at its most uniform, people could still
distinguish status by tailoring, quality of material, and especially shoes.
This is not a unique Chinese response to control of course: Anyone fa-

miliar with school uniforms knows how students still manage to make style and status distinctions among themselves—more subtly than students who need not wear uniforms, but just as clearly. Clothing was just the tip of the iceberg in China, where high rank brought wide ranges of special privileges, from better access to university libraries for full professors to cars and special hospitals for high officials. Even in daily life the body language of hierarchy never faded, with its concern for who sits where, who goes through a door first, and who eats the first bite of food. While many of these hierarchies were defined by the state itself, they also undercut its own Lei Feng ideal of selfhood.

The totalitarian project of a unified identity also failed because the kinds of alternative social networks I just discussed promote a different view of the self. China could not depart from certain basic social structures independent from the state, although it did try to invade them. In particular, they encouraged the family as the best way to socialize children and care for the old, and they fostered neighborhood ties through the housing system. Housing for most peasants remained in the original village structures. For urban residents most people gained access to housing through their work unit, which also controlled many other social resources. While this integrated people into the state hierarchy, it also created a huge set of daily ties and contacts over which the state had little control. In just the same way, its system of small group political meetings empowered those groups, and sometimes allowed them to pursue their own interests. Families, small political study groups, villages, and neighborhoods all undercut the image of the state as a unified body.

The economic reforms of the 1980s have also brought an enormous loosening of the totalitarian attempt to impose an identity. Fashion has blossomed, "comrade" is dying out, and recent campaigns for "civilization" or Lei Feng have had few teeth. When China argues that human rights have in fact greatly increased, they refer especially to these kinds of personal freedoms to craft an individual self, and they are right. People have clearly jumped at the opportunity, and are now far more differentiated by consumption than before 1980.

This change is not just the embrace of Western-style individualistic consumerism, although that is part of the picture. It also shows up in the revival of uniquely Chinese ideas of self. The resurgence of the arts of *qi* manipulation in the People's Republic is a clear example. *Qi*, a kind of vital energy, flows through everything. Health and good fortune stem from keeping the quality and quantity of various kinds of *qi* balanced. Chinese medicine manipulates the flow of *qi* into the body through diet and herbal medicines, and within the body through acupuncture. Geomancy adjusts the flow of *qi* in the environment to the individuals in it, by carefully siting graves and houses. *Qigong* exercises create health by balancing and enhancing the flow of *qi* in the body through physical movement. Chinese medicine has always thrived in the People's Republic, but *qigong* and geomancy rebounded only in the 1980s. *Qigong* attracted a huge following, officially reaching about 60 million by 1990.[28] Masters claimed to emit powerful heat rays, or to cure by laying on hands. The resurgence of geomancy (which had always remained strong in Taiwan and Hong Kong) is more difficult to document, but the number of articles in internal state and party journals in the last decade devoted to the "problem" of "superstitious practices" among the people and even among Communist Party members leave little room for doubt that traditional ideas are alive and well and even enjoying a resurgence of popularity in the People's Republic. This set of ideas offers a very different sense of self, one rooted in the energy flows of the universe and not the unity of the Chinese state. Perhaps this is one reason the government began to repress the *qigong* movement.[29] Popular worship of deities, which has also increased enormously in the last two decades, also offers an alternative sense of self, although I will leave that discussion for Chapter 6.

Gender also leads to partially divergent identities, and it is no coincidence that the first obvious change in fashion was a strong gender differentiation from roughly unisex dress to women in frills and men in sunglasses. There is no need to reiterate the evidence that women are not truly equal in China, that their revolution was largely postponed.[30] While they did join the workforce in massive numbers, most women continued to bear the primary burden of child care and household chores, and to receive lower rates of pay. The typical pattern of rural residence is still for a new wife to move into her husband's village, where she has few social connections and must develop a new social network. Tensions between a woman's ties to her natal family and those to her husband's family also still remain salient. Women's social networks are thus not entirely the same as men's, and this affects identity. Women's networks tend to be more local than men's, often concerning gifts among neighbors and kin in the context of marriage introductions, helping with a child's education, or rites of passage like weddings and funerals. Women sometimes characterize men's connections as more utilitarian or political.[31] Some kinds of gifts circulate only among women—cloth, for example, may be given to a bride and sewn into a wedding dress by her new mother-in-law.[32] Gifts of food and garden products also typically circulate only among networks of women.[33]

Conclusions

All of this evidence points to the conclusion that the totalitarian project, and authoritarian control more generally, have never succeeded in fully controlling social and cultural life. Nor are they likely to succeed more than partially. This is in part because the attempt to control social life itself creates ties beyond control. The inevitable existence of a second economy under socialism is one example, and so is the necessity for personal connections in such societies. Taiwanese developed similar mechanisms to preserve some local autonomy during their long authoritarian period. Throughout the twentieth century, for example, every move to control the image of the body by enforcing politeness campaigns like Chiang Kai-shek's New Life Movement or by extolling the selfless self via Lei Feng has been met with a disorganized alternative, like the *qigong* exercise craze, which delineates a very different bodily and moral universe. The kinds of horizontal connections that permeated late imperial society were harried, pressured, and compressed, but they survived. Families and sometimes lineages remain strong in all these regimes; so do surname ties, classmate ties, place of origin ties, and religious ties. In some ways, both market and socialist economies have promoted horizontal ties—they are crucial for raising capital in Taiwan, for finding overseas partners and markets in Singapore, and for all those things plus manipulating the remaining socialist system on the mainland. The People's Republic has pushed more effectively on these things than any other Chinese regime, but even they left enough intact throughout their most radical periods to allow a rapid regrowth of these ties when they retreated to a more corporatist model.

Authoritarian control has thus never been fully successful in China, or perhaps anywhere. Such regimes have never ended small-scale informal ties, but they can be powerfully effective in preventing any large-scale civil organizations from forming. Thus the Chinese crushed all signs of incipient independent labor unions after June 4, 1989, even though labor had played only a marginal role. The leadership was struck by the events in Poland just as much as Western scholars of civil society were, and had no intention of allowing any Chinese Solidarity to develop. Mass organizations exist in great numbers, of course, but only when organized through the state and under the control of the Communist Party. No other nonstate organizations are allowed to reach a large scale. The same was largely true of Taiwan until 1987.

While an "informal social sector" of personal ties and alternate identities survives and sometimes thrives under authoritarian control, formal organizations are repressed, incorporated into the state, or at least have their tops cut off. Anthropologists who study kinship often distinguish between corporate and ego-centered kin groups. Corporate groups are usually constructed around descent from a common ancestor, traced only through men or only through women. The unilineal principle makes very clear who is qualified to be a member, since any individual can claim only one group. Such corporate groups work well for holding common property because they define the rights in that property so clearly. The Chinese lineage is a good example. Ego-centered networks typically result instead when kinship is traced through both sides of the family. This creates overlapping groups, where each set of siblings has unique ties and boundaries are hard to draw around distinct groups of relatives. In such situations corporate property rights through kinship do not work clearly, and people create their own networks of kinsmen out of the array available to them. Kinship (as in the United States) becomes a set of social ties that can be mobilized or left to atrophy, unlike corporate kin groups where membership is clear and often carries some kind of property rights.

The distinction is parallel to the kinds of social self-organization possible under authoritarian regimes. Social groups comparable to corporate kin groups were not tolerated, except on a very small scale. Standing groups with clear membership, independent leadership, and control over resources were disbanded or brought under corporate political control. On the other hand, informal networks of ties constructed by individuals thrived. These draw on all kinds of social relations quite separate from the totalizing control imagined by the state. The real question for political transformation is not whether alternative social resources exist in China—we know that they do. Rather, it is when those alternatives can coalesce into something able to exert political pressure.

As I will discuss in the chapters that follow, this transformation happened very quickly in Taiwan after martial law was lifted. The state created free space for such organizations for the first time, and they quickly formed out of existing informal social relations. The situation in the People's Republic is considerably more complex. Much more space has opened at the personal level, but large, formally organized, independent social organizations remain effectively impossible. Even without that, however, the informal sector can be very influential. Recent studies, for example, have suggested that peasants played a critical role in pushing the state toward the economic reforms beginning in the late 1970s. The initial reforms explicitly discouraged households from entering directly into agricultural contracts with the commune—the "household responsibility system" that would later take China by storm.[34] Yet peasants, especially in Anhui and Sichuan, went ahead on their own initiative, drawing on their own very local social resources. Bottom-level cadres often colluded with them to disguise what they were doing, in the interests of raising their crop yields. Local conspiracies

> came together spontaneously and without plan. Authority was challenged only at the level of the most humble officials; wherever possible, peasants

defused even that small confrontation by engaging the local cadres in collusion. . . . Peasants made up names of bogus new organizational structures to disguise the dismantling of the collectives. They entered pacts of mutual protection to insure a livelihood for families of arrested conspirators. They twisted policy intentions to get what they wanted and willfully misinterpreted orders. . . . What would ordinarily be construed as peasant resistance became more than resistance. It became a force with the power to shape and create policy.[35]

The forms of personal and social identity that occupied the free space in the Chinese countryside here managed major policy transformations, even without any formal political organization.

The economic reforms of the last fifteen years, by necessity, are creating new forms of formal and informal associations, from chambers of commerce to restaurants like Beijing's Heping Fandian, which tries to cater only to big businessmen.[36] The need to raise capital, find markets, identify business partners, and enforce contracts is fostering a new range of nonstate ties. As the government has gradually let go of the economy, it has also allowed much more room for private activity. Dissent is still not tolerated, but nonpolitical organizations are beginning to thrive for the first time in decades. I begin to explore this in the chapter that follows.

Notes

1. David Strand, *Rickshaw Beijing: City People and Politics in the 1920s* (Berkeley: University of California Press, 1989), p. 168.

2. Tang Zhenchang, "Civil Consciousness and Shanghai Society," *Social Sciences in China* (Spring 1995), p. 71.

3. Michel Foucault, *Discipline and Punish: The Birth of the Prison*, trans. Alan Sheridan (New York: Vintage, 1979), pp. 195–228.

4. See, for example, Putnam, "Bowling Alone."

5. See, for example, Hannah Arendt, *The Origins of Totalitarianism*, 2d ed. (Cleveland: World Publishing, 1958); and Claude Lefort, *The Political Forms of Modern Society: Bureaucracy, Democracy, Totalitarianism*, ed. John B. Thompson (Cambridge, Mass.: MIT Press, 1986).

6. See Arif Dirlik, "The Ideological Foundations of the New Life Movement: A Study in Counterrevolution," *Journal of Asian Studies* 34(4) (1975), pp. 945–80.

7. New Life Road is still a major Taipei thoroughfare.

8. See Tien Hung-mao, *The Great Transition: Political and Social Change in the Republic of China* (Stanford: Hoover Institution Press, 1989), especially Chapter 3 on interest groups.

9. See also Thomas B. Gold, "Civil Society in Taiwan: The Confucian Dimension," in Wei-ming Tu, ed., *Confucian Traditions*, pp. 244–258.

10. On factions see Tsai Ming-hui and Chang Mau-kuei, "Formation and Transformation of Local *P'ai-hsi*: A Case Study of Ho-k'ou Town," *Bulletin of the Insti-*

tute of Ethnology, Academia Sinica 77 (1994), pp. 125–156; Joseph Bosco, "Taiwan Factions: *Guanxi*, Patronage and the State in Local Politics," *Ethnology* 31(2) (1992), pp. 157–83; Shelley Rigger, "Electoral Strategies and Political Institutions in the Republic of China on Taiwan," Fairbank Center Working Papers, no. 1, Cambridge Mass., 1993.

11. This discussion is based on Edwin A. Winckler, "Cultural Policy on Postwar Taiwan," in Harrell and Huang, eds., *Cultural Change*, pp. 22–46.

12. Kenneth Dean gives a comparable example of the survival of a local god procession in Fujian under difficult political circumstances in the People's Republic in his book, *Taoist Ritual and Popular Cults of Southeast China* (Princeton: Princeton University Press, 1993), pp. 99–117.

13. George L. Mackay, *From Far Formosa: The Island, Its People and Missions*, 4th ed. (New York: Fleming H. Revell, 1895), pp. 130–131.

14. Suzuki Seichiro, *Taiwan Jiuguan Xisu Xinyang [Old Customs and Traditional Beliefs of Taiwan]*, trans. Gao Jianzhi and Feng Zuomin (Taipei: Zhongwen, 1978[1934]), p. 473.

15. Weller, *Unities and Diversities*, pp. 80–81.

16. Ibid., pp. 138–139.

17. See Taiwan Sheng Wenxian Weiyuanhui, comp., *Taiwan Sheng Tongzhi [Complete Gazetteer of Taiwan Province]* (Taipei: Zhongwen, 1980), pp. 292–295.

18. P. Steven Sangren, "A Chinese Marketing Community: An Historical Ethnography of Ta-Ch'i, Taiwan" (Ph.D. diss., Stanford University, 1979), p. 131.

19. See Weller, *Unities and Diversities*, pp. 140–142.

20. Some areas also decollectivized this land during the first half of the Cultural Revolution.

21. See Katerhine Verdery, "Theorizing Socialism: A Prologue to the 'Transition,'" *American Ethnologist* 18(3) (1991), p. 422; Vivienne Shue, *The Reach of the State: Sketches of the Chinese Body Politic* (Stanford: Stanford University Press, 1988), p. 110; István R. Gábor, "Modernity or a New Kind of Duality? Second Thoughts on the "Second Economy" (paper presented at the conference on the Obstacles to the Transformation of Soviet-type Societies in Eastern Europe, Vienna, 1991), photocopy.

22. Yunxiang Yan, *The Flow of Gifts: Reciprocity and Social Networks in a Chinese Village* (Stanford: Stanford University Press, 1996), pp. 76–77.

23. See, for example, Andrew B. Kipnis, *Producing Guanxi: Sentiment, Self, and Subculture in a North China Village* (Durham, N.C.: Duke University Press, 1997); and Mayfair Mei-hui Yang, *Gifts, Favors and Banquets: The Art of Social Relationships in China* (Ithaca, N.Y.: Cornell University Press, 1994). Yang in particular argues that this world of connections is so powerful as to constitute a polity of its own (p. 308).

24. Shu-min Huang, *The Spiral Road: Changes in a Chinese Village Through the Eyes of a Communist Party Leader* (Boulder: Westview Press, 1989), p. 145. The study also contains other similar examples (e.g., pp. 69, 136, 143).

25. Anita Chan, Richard Madsen, and Jonathon Unger, *Chen Village under Mao and Deng*, 2d ed. (Berkeley: University of California Press, 1992). There is a similar case from a village near Beijing in Norman A. Chance, *China's Urban Villagers: Changing Life in a Beijing Suburb*, 2d ed. (Fort Worth, Tax.: Holt, Rinehart and Win-

ston, 1991), pp. 50–51. See also Jean Oi, *State and Peasant in Contemporary China* (Berkeley: University of California Press, 1989).

26. Ann S. Anagnost, *National Past-times: Narrative, Writing, and History in Modern China* (Durham, N.C.: Duke University Press, 1997).

27. See Lefort, *The Political Forms of Modern Society*, p. 299; and Robert P. Weller, *Resistance, Chaos and Control in China: Taiping Rebels, Taiwanese Ghosts and Tiananmen* (London: Macmillan, 1994), p. 214.

28. Nicholas D. Kristof, "A Mystical Art, but Can It Make the Lame Walk?" *New York Times*, 4 September 1990, p. A4.

29. See also Nancy Chen, "Mystics, Millenarians and *Mixin*" (paper presented at the annual meeting of the Association for Asian Studies, Boston, 1994).

30. See Margery Wolf, *Revolution Postponed: Women in Contemporary China* (Stanford: Stanford University Press, 1985).

31. Yang, *Gifts, Favors and Banquets*, p. 81–82.

32. Kipnis, *Producing Guanxi*, pp. 71–72.

33. Yan, *The Flow of Gifts*, p. 65.

34. Daniel Kelliher, *Peasant Power in China: The Era of Rural Reform, 1979–1989* (New Haven: Yale University Press, 1992), especially pp. 60–64.

35. Ibid., p. 104.

36. See David L. Wank, "Private Business, Bureaucracy, and Political Alliance in a Chinese City," *Australian Journal of Chinese Affairs* 33 (1995), pp. 55–71, on chambers of commerce.

4

Business and the Limits to Civil Association

In a market-based economy businesses and businessmen need to organize. They do this in part because they need to lobby the government—they may want lower taxes, or tariffs on competing imported goods, or tougher labor laws. Different businesses may have conflicting interests, and these groups will not always speak with a single voice. This also encourages them to organize to make themselves heard. Businesses also associate in part because they rely on various informal ties of trust and friendship for credit, marketing ties, information, and other business needs. The results are things like Lions clubs and Rotarians in addition to chambers of commerce. Informal association in clubs and restaurants is just as important. Business organizations are thus an obvious place to look for democratic civility—what role did they play in Taiwan's political transition, and how are they developing in the new market environment of the People's Republic? The evidence I will discuss suggests that they are not particularly effective because big business is so closely integrated with the state. In addition, authoritarian governments have effectively limited organization in the formal sector. While I argued in the previous chapter for inherent limits to authoritarian control, this chapter shows the limits on civil self-organization in such systems.

The role of business associations in a potentially alternative East Asian democratic civility raises a related problem—is there an alternative East Asian capitalism, and why have various Chinese societies been so successful in the market economy? Arguments about Chinese economic culture resemble the arguments about civil and political culture I discussed in Chapter 1. In both cases Chinese culture appears either irrelevant, washed along by the tides of the market, or omnipotent, broadly preadapting the region for a kind of "Confucian" capitalism.[1] These arguments about what has come to be called "post-Confucianism" have received more attention than the role of culture in civil associations, and so they are worth a closer look.[2]

The list of most important "post-Confucian" features usually includes an emphasis on human relations and social harmony based on the idea of filial piety, respect for authority and strong identity with the organization, and a combination of worldly diligence and fatalism.[3] The contrast with Western individualist atomization is implicit throughout. All but the most naive authors, of course, would admit that this simplifies a great deal of social, geographic, and historical variation. Yet they would also insist (and I would agree) that, on the whole, some such set of ideas and practices does in fact usefully differentiate the Chinese and Western cultural spheres. While it is certainly possible to trace these views, however loosely defined, back to the thought of Confucius himself, they also pervade many aspects of Chinese culture generally, even among people who could say nothing of philosophical Confucianism.

This general description of Chinese culture has shaped Western understandings of the growth of Asian market economies throughout the twentieth century. Alarmingly, however, the conclusions social scientists now draw from these features are just the opposite of what people concluded from the same observations for the first sixty or seventy years of the century. From Weber's original pessimistic predictions through the modernization theorists of the 1950s and 1960s, the standard arguments considered Chinese culture inimical to capitalism. Weber himself had argued that the Confucian "enchanted world" did not create the drive toward change that allowed Protestantism to catalyze the European economic transformation, and that Chinese "sib fetters" further hampered the market.[4] Others argued that family-centered particularism blocked rational economic development, or that China had religious impediments to economic growth.[5] Now, however, these very features are offered as the keys to East Asian economic success.[6] This reevaluation of Chinese culture does not represent any theoretical breakthrough, but instead stems from a belated recognition of the empirical facts of successful development.[7]

In retrospect, the problems with the earlier version seem clear. Earlier analyses treated Chinese culture as an abstract, clearly formulated set of propositions, often based on Chinese elite descriptions of their cultural ideals. From these, one read off social and economic consequences based on difference from an equally idealized version of Western market culture. Instead of placing actual behavior in real contexts, they assumed an automatic translation of a unitary culture into action. The new version, in part because Chinese scholars have taken the lead in its development, grounds its claims in a far better understanding of Chinese culture and history. It also has the good fortune of coming after the fact, and so will not suffer the kind of empirical disproof that awaited the modernization version.

The new version of Chinese culture is thus much deeper than the old one, but continues to offer a unitary culture largely out of context. Its post facto origins raise the danger of picking only those bits of traditional China most clearly preadapted to capitalism, and ignoring the equally interesting question of how its many ill-adapted features have been overcome. Imperial China, after all, included a number of quite different cultural currents. Neo-Confucianism had the blessing of the state, but other sets of ideas also played important roles, even among the elite. The diversity of Chinese culture meant that it was not simply preadapted (or ill-adapted, in older readings) to a new economic system, but that it reacted differentially to historical events. Chinese have thrived in market economies because they have successfully mined and refined some aspects of their cultural resources, and successfully buried others.[8] There is an alternative Chinese-style capitalism with roots in Chinese culture, but the culture itself has also changed in the process. We can expect much the same to be true for civil associations, leaving open the real possibility of alternative democratic civilities built on East Asian cultures.

Out of context, features like respect for authority might be expected to suffocate entrepreneurial creativity (the old line, still occasionally heard about Japan) as easily as to guarantee labor peace and corporate harmony (the new line). In practice, respect for authority looks less important in Chinese societies than one might have predicted. Employees in fact tend to learn the ropes and then split off to compete with their old employers: they get out from under authority as quickly as they can. As the Taiwanese cliché goes, it is better to be a chicken's beak than a bull's behind. The metaphor of the firm as family thus runs into immediate limits, although managers often make the comparison.[9] This conclusion, of course, also limits the importance of a culture of authority in building democracy.

In much the same way, extensive reliance on particularistic ties opens the door to corruption and graft, even as it eases problems of capital formation, marketing, and employee loyalty. The Chinese talent for the market lies less in their ability to draw on social networks than in their ability to prevent those networks from bleeding them dry. Does family loyalty create a high achievement motivation, or encourage disloyalty to others? Over two millennia ago the legalist Han Feizi attacked Confucian family loyalty for implying disloyalty to the state. If children had a duty to preserve their bodies to serve their parents, who would fight the wars? Modernization theorists were not wrong to emphasize the dangers of particularistic ties (as nearly any Chinese entrepreneur will attest); their mistake was to ignore real mechanisms for dealing with those dangers, and to assume the inevitability of convergence toward Western market rationality.[10]

Arguments about the role of Chinese culture in their current economic success have thus moved beyond a monolithic view of culture. They have managed this in part by looking beyond the formal economic sector to the actual ties that influence daily economic life, which may not have the blessing of either legal codification or elite ideology. The informal social sector, based on networks of personal connections (*guanxi*), has been crucial to economic success in Chinese East Asia. Broadening the idea of an "informal economic sector" (beyond state regulatory and legal control, but not necessarily illegal), this chapter addresses both the informal and formal social sectors in Chinese business, and their relations to the state. The social ties that have been crucial for market success in China and Taiwan are also the raw material for civil association. I thus include both formally organized and recognized associations (chambers of commerce, business federations, Rotary clubs) and the kinds of informal ties that can be just as important.

Social Embeddedness

The informal social sector always exists, but it thrives in the economy especially where legal controls are weak. Powerfully corporatist systems (like the People's Republic today and Taiwan before 1987) leave very little legal space for formal associations independent from the state. As a result business in both places relies heavily on informal personal ties to other businesses and to individuals in government. The nature of these personal ties and the ways people pull them together have roots in the kinds of interpersonal connections that have long existed in China, but they must also adapt to the needs of the market. We understand these processes best in Taiwan, so I will begin there.

While Taiwan's government often indulged in repressive tactics and campaigned for control of body and mind, it left the economy much less tied to the state than in the People's Republic. Certain kinds of civil association familiar in the West thus arose fairly early in Taiwan, partly through contact with the West. Rotary clubs, Lions clubs, and other standard forms of association have a long history there. Such associations thrived in Taiwan only partially in emulation of the West. They also reinforce the older kinds of connections (kinship, common place of origin, classmate), whose role in Taiwan's business success has now been clearly documented.[11] Such groups have increasingly played an important role in promoting political change in Taiwan, especially concerning relations with the mainland in the last few years. The lifting of martial law in 1987 allowed big business to exert new leverage on the state, and businessmen are coming to dominate elected bodies the way lawyers do in the United States.[12]

The Taiwanese government has promoted large enterprises since the 1950s, but left most other people to their own economic devices.[13] Banks, for example, would only make loans where there was sufficient collateral. This made bank credit, with all its legal guarantees, impossible for most small entrepreneurs. In addition, financial information tended to be opaque, and accounting standards were inconsistent and not well enforced. The problem was not so much in the legal framework for the economy as in passing such idealistic and strict legal codes that officials simply could not enforce them. As a lawyer studying the issue put it:

> The stilted and narrow perspective implicit in much ROC legislation does not disrupt the social order in Taiwan when it is ignored, as it is much of the time. . . . To a considerable extent, the small and medium-sized businesses, which still constitute the greater part of Taiwan's economy, have operated free from central government interference. Lax enforcement of tax, labor, environmental protection, and zoning laws meant that small businesses operated with considerable autonomy but little support from the central government.[14]

A system like this forces even big businesses to rely on personal trust for basic financial information about other businesses. Small operators were pushed to develop their own mechanisms. They found start-up capital, for example, through kinsmen, neighbors, and friends. They had to rely on informal credit arrangements based on their personal connections, including especially rotating credit associations and post-dated checks. Perhaps 30 to 40 percent of the financial resources of private enterprises in Taiwan comes from such informal mechanisms.[15]

These systems have worked effectively in Taiwan, but all rely on personal trust instead of the institutionalized and impersonal trust of an effective legal system. Trust (*xinyong*, which also means credit) must be judged from the past behavior of known individuals, and Taiwanese draw on their repertoire of personal connections that I discussed in Chapter 2—relations of kinship and marriage, common place of origin, classmate ties, and so on. The result is what Winn calls a system of "relational capital." We can easily see traces of it by following out the wide and amorphous personal networks that unite business groups in Taiwan.[16] Gary Hamilton's study of the 743 firms in Taiwan's 96 largest business groups found that every single firm had co-owners, including both kinsmen and unrelated personal connections. He concludes that horizontal networks of personal connections form the "organizational backbone of the manufacturing sectors of the economy."[17] At a much

lower level of Taiwanese society, interpersonal ties also shape the sub-
contracting system for garment construction in a Taipei neighborhood.[18]
These studies leave no doubt that ties of family, marriage, neighborhood,
and all the rest play a central role in Chinese business. They imply a clear
contrast with an idealized version of rationalized Western market culture, where contractual ties between separate individuals supposedly
substitute for personalistic ties of trust. By some estimates, less than 2
percent of Taiwanese firms are large businesses, and one of every eight
Taiwanese adults is a "boss." The resulting structure is equally different
from the state-driven huge business conglomerates of Japan or South
Korea, which have quite different cultural and political roots.[19]

If we turn to the People's Republic during the last two decades of reform, we see a very similar pattern of informal social connections at the
local level.[20] Like Taiwan before 1987, these have no legal or ideological
protection, but are allowed to thrive almost unmolested as long as they
keep away from open politics and do not try to move into the formal sector. Large businesses tend to have close ties to the state bureaucracy,
while the small ones fend for themselves. Again as in Taiwan, bank credit
is almost impossible for small borrowers, who must draw on the same
sets of personal ties as their compatriots across the Strait—kinsmen,
classmates, rotating credit associations, and the rest of the informal sector.

Small entrepreneurs (*geti hu,* "individual households," which legally
have fewer than eight employees) in the People's Republic live and die
on their personal networks. Small entrepreneurs generally lack good connections to officials, and initially often had "bad" class backgrounds and
thus poor political connections. Family ties were one of the only effective
resources available to them. The major sources of capital for entrepreneurs, in order of importance, are personal savings, loans from relatives
and other connections, and pooled resources. Bank loans are a distant
fourth because they are so hard to get, much like the situation in Taiwan.[21] One result of people's need to broaden their personal networks to
succeed in the market has been a shift in the uses of kinship. The usual
expectations of patriliny in China are giving way to a cognatic system, at
least in cities, where people construct networks of relatives chosen
equally through men and women.[22] On the other hand, larger businesses
(*siying qiye,* "private enterprises"), which almost invariably have close
ties to the state, use family ties much less. They often express their suspi-
cion of kinship ties as leading to abuse of the relationship, or as simply
not being "scientific."[23]

The glue that holds these personal networks together is gift-giving.
Yan Yunxiang's detailed study of these networks found that fully 20 percent of a typical rural household budget went for gifts, and that this fig-

ure had increased generally since 1949 and especially after decollectivization in the area in 1984.[24] The predominant place of gifts in household budgets shows the extent to which networks must be constructed and actively maintained. These may be "personalistic" ties of family and neighborhood, but they must be actively nurtured. If being born to such ties was enough, people would not have to invest so much in them.

Yan found that many gifts were expressive rather than instrumental, but villagers also clearly distinguished purely utilitarian categories of gifts: flatteries (*liuxu*), lubrications (*shangyou*) in exchange for future favors, and indirect payments (which appear as expressive gifts to people outside one's usual network) in exchange for favors already received. In the world of business, the line between gift and bribe can easily blur. Government officials themselves often have the widest networks, and so most successfully make the move to private business. All large businesses must cultivate state officials, just as all small ones cultivate social networks. In interviews, managers just saw this as part of the cost of business. One said: "We hate so-called 'upright officials.' Those people don't take your money, but they don't do their duties as officials either. They are worse than corrupt officials. We have no way at all to deal with 'upright officials' because they will not help you in any sense." Similar findings occurred in Xiamen, where small businesses usually deeply resented bribes they had to pay officials, while large businesses considered it normal.[25]

Taiwan and the People's Republic still run on very different economic principles. The combined economy of the People's Republic has encouraged the higher level of corruption there by leaving so much economic power in the hands of the state. Without a strong rule of law, entrepreneurs must turn to personal means to function. The People's Republic has also allowed even less independent business organization than Taiwan did before 1987. Perhaps most important of all, the economic power remaining under the control of officials has led to an increasing blurring of the line between the bureaucratic and market economies, where officials act as quasi-public entrepreneurs, and entrepreneurs have quasi-private official backers.[26]

The differences between China and Taiwan, however, make some fundamental similarities stand out strikingly. First, the market economy in both is loosely split between big companies with strong legal support and personal ties to the state, and small firms that have thrived largely because they are left alone by the state. These small fry neither enjoy benefits like access to credit or legal protections of formal contracts, nor suffer from the fetters of being closely supervised. Second, business relations in both places are firmly embedded in the informal social sector, especially for those many small businesses that cannot expect much help from the state. This is the heart of the claim for a uniquely Chinese modernity.

Two problems, however, prevent us from simply declaring that Chinese societies have established an alternative to Western market culture, and may therefore also establish an alternative civil culture. The first is that the picture of Western business practice on which the contrast relies is itself "occidentalized." Family business, for example, drove early Western capitalism in much the same way as people have recently documented for Chinese society today. While there has been a gradual (but by no means complete) move away from that model, it may suggest that family-centered capitalism works well during the early development of market economies. If so, then the Chinese evidence may describe an earlier stage of capitalism rather than a true alternative.[27]

The second problem, clearly related to the first, is that these Chinese economies continue to change very rapidly. With the passing of several decades of continuous development, business in Taiwan and Hong Kong is only now beginning to face some of the difficulties that might discourage the family model and the extensive use of personalistic ties: small family enterprises are becoming large firms, labor-intensive production is moving to the high technology and service sectors, company founders are searching for successors, and economic growth elsewhere in Asia is creating a more fiercely competitive marketplace. Indeed, some new evidence suggests that people are relying less than ever on traditional interpersonal connections, and that the quality of such relations is becoming progressively thinner. Several studies have suggested a dilution of the human feelings (*renqing*) implied in relationships in the People's Republic since market-oriented economic reforms began in the early 1980s, and the growth of more purely utilitarian ties.[28] Many entrepreneurs now explicitly reject the use of kinship ties as old-fashioned, and prefer more "modern" relationships, for instance with classmates. Managers of larger enterprises in the People's Republic particularly like to emphasize their commitment to "scientific" management. This pattern is especially true for younger entrepreneurs in the information and service sectors.[29]

The situation remains very much in flux, yet the Chinese have clearly drawn on their cultural traditions to address new economic opportunities. Chinese values do affect management behavior, and business activity relies heavily on ties established outside the market. The lack of state support for the small business sector that is so important in both Taiwan and the People's Republic, along with the authoritarian discouragement of independent business organizations, forced small businesses into the informal sector. There they have thrived by drawing on uniquely Chinese cultural resources.

The Role of Women

In a typically Confucian way, much of the literature on Chinese culture and business ties assumes that there are no women, or at best that there are no differences between men and women. If true, this would be surprising indeed. We now have two decades of studies of family and gender clearly showing that women's interests in their families and their views of those fundamental kin relationships at the core of Confucian thought differed significantly from their husbands, fathers, and sons. Women's work was in theory confined to the domestic sphere; even when they produced commodities, men mediated access to the market.[30] As I discussed in Chapter 2, wives had no direct access to their husbands' personal networks, and their own external contacts were confined to their natal families and to other women of their husbands' villages. Women also had little reason to share their husbands' view of the family as one link in an infinite chain of patrilineal connections. While most wives dutifully burned incense every morning for their husbands' ancestors, they did not worship their own ancestors. Even if a woman's parents had no other descendants to worship them, her husband's family would probably begrudge their tablets only a dusty corner in a back room.[31] Women instead focused on creating a "uterine family."[32] The birth of a son in particular would solidify her place in her husband's house; fostering his continuing loyalty would protect her in the years to come.

McEwen documents a nice example in Hong Kong, where a group of brothers extols the virtues of family business and Chinese culture, while their sister is distinctly less enthusiastic about the paternalistic model. One of the brothers explains the superiority of family business: "Maybe it is difficult for Western people, but for the Chinese people it is very easy for us to get along. Even though we have the Western education, we have traditional customs we all follow, that is the reason why the British lose and Hong Kong is so successful. [The British] made a mess of the UK; only the Chinese people can do [family business]."

The sister, however, says that: "For me, I don't like to be in the family business. . . . When you have the family business, you cannot have a good business, or a good relationship with the brothers. . . . If I can work for outside, and something is unhappy, then we can have an argument, it is easy to handle and we can start being partners again. But if you are unhappy with your family, . . . it's better to be separate."[33]

Women had their own resources that would become relevant to the market. While women's spheres of connections were much smaller than men's, they could also be more reliable. Her own natal family had the advantage of being trustworthy, but also socially distant enough to prevent them becoming a drain if problems arose. In addition, the close ties uniting village networks of women could make up for the limited scale of the group. Women thus make extensive use of rotating credit associations. One study found that women in Henan, Zhejiang, and Fujian made up 64 percent of all entrepreneurs participating in rotating credit associations.[34] These have been one of the most important ways of raising entrepreneurial capital, but they rely on high degrees of trust because it is so easy to abscond with all the funds.[35] The closeness of women's networks may help them establish the necessary kinds of ties, while men may have broader but more utilitarian ties more open to abuse. As I have mentioned, kinship ties through women are also becoming increasingly important for small business in China.

Many women have become entrepreneurs in Hong Kong, Taiwan, and the People's Republic. The legislated end of foot-binding (and other legal changes, especially in marriage rights) early in the century, much greater access to education, opportunities for wage labor, and other changes have helped open the market directly to women. Some estimate that fully half of the petty entrepreneurs in the People's Republic are women.[36] Men still dominate, however, and very few women run manufacturing businesses. Research with nineteen women entrepreneurs in Tianjin showed that they tended to be older, enter business more recently, and have less education than men in comparable businesses.[37] All of the businesses are small-scale, and many of the women began their businesses because they were laid off by state firms—a growing phenomenon that generally affects women before men.

Family can pose a major problem for women entrepreneurs. They continue to face responsibility for providing their husbands with sons, and for taking care of children and household. Young women in particular may have to choose between family and career, and preliminary evidence suggests a high divorce rate for such women.[38] At the same time, young female entrepreneurs value the new freedoms of their position, and its opportunities for self-fulfillment.[39]

Many of these career women feel cut off from the male world of connections. They particularly miss the opportunity to cement ties through the endless banqueting in which men indulge. Some of this takes place in hostess bars, in which the women feel uncomfortable, and most of it involves competitive social drinking, in which women have traditionally not been welcome. Taking part in such events would call the woman's character into question. Rumors also follow women who must travel for their business, and the endless rumors were one of the major complaints of the women interviewed in Tianjin. Some women deal with this problem by going into business with their husbands. More creatively, some women use their sons or brothers as fronts at public events. They remain backstage pulling the strings, while their men work the male networks. One woman in Tianjin relies completely on her husband, who is, conveniently, a police officer, to maintain her business network. Another has her husband make all her deliveries in his taxi.[40] They thus continue to make use of ties of uterine and natal family, running the business as "inside people," just as they ran the family. Some women also point to their gender as an advantage—they say that men are more willing to do things for them without expensive gifts, and that men also do not want to lose face by fighting with women.[41]

These women draw on traditional family skills of kin management to succeed; they also turn traditional gender stereotypes to their advantage. Women must generally forge their own networks. Some draw on traditional ties to do this, as when they raise capital through a rotating credit association of old friends. Others, like men, cultivate ties to the state-owned economy that they usually developed in earlier jobs. Sixteen of the nineteen women interviewed in Tianjin kept formal affiliations with their earlier state-owned units for the benefit of their current private business. Some women, however, simply start from scratch by searching out like-minded people. One young woman, for example, needed a business partner in Taiwan. She had no connections at all, and no way of manipulating a network to create some. She resorted instead to looking people up in the phone book, where she finally found some equally unconnected partners—young people whose study abroad had cut them off from traditional networks—with compatible business interests.[42] This use of less personalistic kinds of ties does not differ fundamentally from the kinds of changes young men are also advancing. In this case, however, women's relative lack of access to the opportunities that traditional ties create for men has led them to promote something more like a Weberian version of rational market behavior.

As with men, women draw on both the traditional resources available to them and on innovative kinds of ties. In the process they set loose a series of contradictory processes—affirming the woman's role in the uterine family but making real family life problematic, drawing on traditionally female ties and skills but promoting a more utilitarian kind of relationship network. Women and men both survive in business by cultivating the informal social sector. The specific ties they draw on, however, partially differ because their relations to earlier moral systems of family and community were not identical. For men, business fits neatly into ideas about the infinite extension of a patriline, because fathers have a duty to provide for the prosperity of future generations of male heirs. Women's roots in smaller scale, more informal networks (as in the rotating credit associations), along with their ability to improvise other kinds of ties when needed, gives them some different civil resources from their husbands. I will examine some of the significance of this for democratic change in the concluding chapter.

State Embeddedness

I have discussed how Chinese and Taiwanese businesses are firmly embedded in informal social networks. It is just as important to understand how they are embedded in the state, because that has equally strong consequences for the development of a democratic civility. Both the People's Republic and Taiwan before its democratization used effective corporatist strategies—creating officially controlled business organizations and stamping out self-organized groups—to keep the informal sector from becoming formally organized and independent.

Taiwan, of course, always allowed much more freedom of economic action than the People's Republic, but the state-owned sector was initially very large in Taiwan too, and is still significant. The state penetrated key sectors like petroleum, electricity, steel, and banking, and the Nationalist Party itself owned another fifty large firms.[43] Even for strictly private business, ties to officials were crucial if an entrepreneur wanted to grow very large in a domestic market protected by the state's industrial policies. It is no surprise that big business in Taiwan never challenged the government politically; the changes that occurred in 1987 had their roots elsewhere.[44]

Both Taiwan (especially before 1987) and the People's Republic (very much still today) promoted corporatist business associations that they could control. All big businesses in Taiwan were organized into sectoral organizations, and workers into official unions. Smaller firms were left alone, although any signs of independent labor or business organization would be co-opted or crushed.[45] The People's Republic, as one might expect, has an even more thorough organization. Independent studies of business associations in Beijing, Tianjin, and Xiamen, as well as interviews with entrepreneurs in 1993 found that the only business associations are arms of the state.[46] China typically creates one kind of organization for petty entrepreneurs and another for larger private businesses. The much closer ties of big businesses to state officials often gives their organization some lobbying power, and allows it—carefully—to articulate some of their interests. In Beijing, for example, the association of bigger businesses campaigned quietly against the government's policy of squeezing credit in 1994.[47] Petty entrepreneurs are organized more thoroughly from the top down, often by officials who see themselves simply as instruments of state policy and who have little sympathy for the businesses they supervise. The result is that smaller businesses try to avoid government bureaucrats, while larger ones play up the connections.

Much of the new market sector in the People's Republic, especially the larger firms, is tightly linked to branches of the state. Large-scale business is simply impossible in China without intimate ties to officials. Indeed, state units run their own semiprivate sideline businesses to make money (schools run factories instead of sponsoring bake sales; the army was running nightclubs), officials often moonlight in business, and many business men and women are ex-officials. A steel factory in Sichuan where I conducted some research in 1997, for example, had spawned a legally independent share-holding company appropriately named the "Enterprise Company." The shares in this company were held by top management from the state-owned company, and the leadership overlapped. The Enterprise Company competed directly with its state-owned parent in some lines of business, relying on the marketing connections of the state bureaucracy, but funneling the profit into the private sector. It also sold services (like cleaning) back to the parent company, while relying on subsidized health care and education from its parent. It was turning a very nice profit (and so were its share-holders), even though the original state-owned company was slowly going bankrupt.

In the absence of a full market economy, the state still controls key resources and contracts. In the absence of an independent legal system, connections (to officials, to hoodlums, or both) are the only guarantors. Children of high cadres have been gobbled up by large firms, including foreign firms, hoping to cement their connections. Thus even where large businesses have no direct and obvious ties to the state, they thrive only by having close and cooperative contacts with officials.

Large firm owners and managers often have close personal connections to officials, but they also have agendas of their own to pursue; they are not simply pawns of officialdom. This desire to get something from the state is why big firms apparently evade taxes less and pay bribes more than petty entrepreneurs. Large businessmen in the booming southern port of Xiamen, for example, did not particularly complain about corruption in 1989, even though it was the driving issue behind that year's demonstrations.[48] We could hardly expect big business associations to oppose the state. It is not in their financial interests as long as the state controls so much of the economy. In addition, of course, no oppositional business organization would be allowed to continue. Small entrepreneurs, on the other hand, do not have the connections to get much from the government, and so see it as interfering at best and voraciously greedy at worst. They deeply resent paying bribes, and try to evade legitimate taxation as well—their fruit stalls and shoe repair shops could not hope to compete with big businesses for lucrative connections, and they stand to gain more by becoming invisible.

None of these ties among businesses thus looks much like civil society. The only ties really independent of the state must remain in the informal sector, and the only formal organizations are fully integrated into the state project. Yet much of this information also points to the limits of state control. The petty entrepreneurs who have been at the heart of the flourishing market in both Taiwan and the People's Republic in practice escape most state scrutiny. They cannot form an explicitly political voice or an independent formal organization, but they can influence policy indirectly. This happened in Taiwan, for example, when the enormous amount of petty trade with the mainland helped lever the government eventually to legalize economic contacts across the Taiwan Strait. Farmers in the People's Republic, who have functioned much like petty entrepreneurs since the economic reforms, also had a strong influence on the policy of decollectivization—never directly, but more often by skirting official directives.[49]

Larger businesses are more careful to cultivate the state, but they will also try to influence policy more directly. In addition to gentle lobbying by their trade organizations, some business leaders get appointed to local consultative committees, and others put informal pressure on local political cadres. One entrepreneur, at a dinner with a township official, openly complained: "We pay taxes! When the government wants something you just come to us and ask for donations. The government thinks all we know is grabbing money; they don't invite us to attend any meetings."[50] This led to an awkward end to the dinner, but it shows the kind of informal pressures that business may create on government. The logic of the market itself can also create pressure to create formal but independent business associations. Gordon Redding, for example, shows how stock markets depend on an independent financial press (to provide investors with information), professional associations to guarantee quality of accountants and lawyers, educational accreditation organizations, and self-policing stock exchange councils.[51] The Chinese government may try to provide these essential services directly, but its own enormous direct and indirect investment in the economy creates a potentially disastrous conflict of interest. Multinationals will also actively push for such associations as independent entities to protect their own business interests. The odds of true independence, however, do not look good now, and there is no evidence that the big business sector will act as a force for democratization.[52]

Taiwan, under similar kinds of pressures, evolved a set of quasi-business associations that escaped corporatist control. These included branches of international legal and accounting associations, and especially organizations like the Junior Chamber of Commerce, Rotary, and Lions clubs, whose international ties helped keep the state at bay.[53] As I will discuss in the chapters that follow, these are the kinds of organizations—not explicitly designed as business associations—that were more important in Taiwan's democratic transition. The same kind of thing has not yet developed strongly in China, although clubs and restaurants that cater to a business clientele fulfill many of the same roles in the informal sector.

Conclusion

Neither the idea of a civil society in dialog with the state nor of an all-encompassing corporatist state captures the dynamics of business association in Taiwan and China. Close ties between private business and government in both places do not look much like civil society. Big business in Taiwan did not play a major role in Taiwan's democracy movement. Big business in Hong Kong similarly cooperated strongly with China before the handover, offering little help to Britain's belated attempt to institutionalize democracy. There is little reason to think anything different is in store in the People's Republic. In addition, the People's Republic continues to be particularly adept at keeping down any independent formal organization of businesses. Business ties are forced into the purely informal sector or into corporatist organizations of the state; there is nothing in between. Taiwan before 1987 was never quite as extreme, and the state was a relatively smaller economic actor, but the basic situation was not so very different. Big business did not push for democratization in Taiwan before 1987, and again did nothing in Hong Kong before 1997. So far, nothing about the People's Republic would lead to any other expectation.

Yet this is also not ideal-typical corporatism, with the social world fully controlled by an authoritarian state. The natural desire of business to influence policy is beginning to create a voice for business in government, even in China. Pressure will also continue to grow from multinationals and indigenous companies for professional associations that can guarantee their investments. Maybe most important of all, however, is the informal social sector in which small businesses particularly thrive. Both Taiwan and the People's Republic have systematically ignored small businesses. Lacking institutional forms of trust, they turn to personal networks for help. The result has been a flowering of social networks independent of the state. These rich, localized, culturally unique ties stem in part from Chinese tradition and history, and in part from the structural isolation of the petty entrepreneurial sector from the state in both Taiwan and China. These are not the kind of thing most writers on civil society think about, but they are the very networks that will be mobilized during times of change.

Notes

1. See Christian Jochim, "Confucius and Capitalism: Views of Confucianism in Works on Confucianism and Economic Development," *Journal of Chinese Religions* 20 (1992), pp. 135–171, for a useful summary of the Chinese language literature on this.

2. The term "post-Confucianism" is used to distinguish these ideas from the millennium-old neo-Confucianism that formed the ideological base of late imperial rule. It is worth recalling, however, that the vast majority of Chinese are Confucian only in the loosest possible sense, and often know nothing of Confucius or later Confucian writers.

3. See Harrell's "Why Do the Chinese Work So Hard?" on the combination of diligence and fatalism. I will not take space here to discuss the combination, which seems counterintuitive, but also reminiscent of Weber's discussion of Calvinism's combination of predestination and a work ethic.

4. Weber, *The Religion of China*.

5. On family see Levy, *The Family Revolution in Modern China*, pp. 354–359; on religion see Bellah, "Epilogue: Religion and Progress in Modern Asia," in Bellah, ed., *Religion and Progress*.

6. See, among many others, Huang Guangguo, "Rujia Lunli yu Qiye Zuzhi Xingtai [Confucian Theory and Types of Enterprise Organization]," in *Zhongguoshi Guanli [Chinese style management]* (Taipei: Gongshang Shibao, 1984), pp. 21–58; Redding, *The Spirit of Chinese Capitalism*; Yang Kuo-shu and Cheng Po-shyun, "Chuantong Jiazhiguan, Geren Xiandaixing ji Zuzhi Xingwei: Hourujia Jiashou de Yixiang Weiguan Yanzheng [Confucianized Values, Individual Modernity, and Organizational Behavior: An Empirical Test of the Post-Confucian Hypothesis]," *Bulletin of the Institute of Ethnology, Academia Sinica* 64 (1987), pp. 1–49; and Yu, *Zhongguo Jinshi Zongjiao Lunli yu Shangren Jingshen [Modern Chinese Religious Ethics and Business Spirit]*.

7. A parallel argument has marked discussion of Chinese immigrants in the United States. Chinese "clannishness," for example, was cited early in the century as a reason that Chinese would never assimilate, and Chinese "timidity" as a reason that they would never be successful entrepreneurs. These cultural features became arguments to halt immigration. By the late twentieth century, however, these same features were read instead as Chinese family loyalty and respect for authority, and cited as reasons for their success in American society. See Tan Hong, "'Orientalism' and Image-making: Chinese Americans as 'Sojourner' and 'Model Minority'" (unpublished, 1986).

8. Not all these useful resources were cultural, of course. Chinese adaptation to a market-driven economy owes just as much to their long history of commercialization, familiarity with cash (Maurice Freedman, "The Handling of Money: A Note on the Background to the Economic Sophistication of Overseas Chinese," *Man* 59 [1959], pp. 64–65), experience with accounting (Robert Gardella, "Squaring Accounts: Commercial Bookkeeping Methods and Capitalist Rationalism in

Late Qing and Republican China," *Journal of Asian Studies* 51[2] [1992], pp. 317–339), and regular use of corporate management (Sangren, "Traditional Chinese Corporations").

9. See Redding, *The Spirit of Chinese Capitalism*.

10. This kind of rationality was never more than an ideal type, after all, even for the West.

11. See Ichiro Numazaki "The Role of Personal Networks in the Making of Taiwan's *Guanxiqiye* ('Related Enterprises')," in Gary G. Hamilton, ed., *Business Networks and Economic Development in East and Southeast Asia* (Hong Kong: Centre of Asian Studies, University of Hong Kong, 1991); and Joseph Bosco, "Family Factories in Taiwan: The Use and Abuse of the Family Metaphor" (paper presented at the annual meeting of the American Anthropological Association, Atlanta, 1994).

12. See Hsin-Huang Michael Hsiao, "The State and Business Relations in Taiwan," *Journal of Far Eastern Business* 1(3) (1995), pp. 76–97.

13. Ibid.

14. Jane Kaufman Winn, "Not by Rule of Law: Mediating State-society Relations in Taiwan Through the Underground Economy," in Murray A. Rubenstein, ed., *The Other Taiwan: 1945 to the Present* (New York: M. E. Sharpe, 1994), p. 186.

15. Ibid., p. 198.

16. See Numazaki, "The Role of Personal Networks," in Hamilton, ed., *Business Networks*.

17. Gary G. Hamilton, "Culture and Organization in Taiwan's Market Economy," in Robert W. Hefner, ed., *Market Cultures: Society and Morality in the New Asian Capitalisms* (Boulder: Westview Press, 1997), p. 64.

18. These are traced in impressive detail in Ka Chih-ming, "Chengxiang Yimin, Xiaoxing Qiye yu Dushi Fei Zhengshi Jingji zhi Xingcheng [Rural Migrants in the City, Small Enterprises and the Formation of the Urban Informal Economy]" (paper presented at the Workshop on Enterprises, Social Relations, and Cultural Practices: Studies of Chinese Societies, Taipei, 1992).

19. See Susan McEwen, "Markets, Modernization, and Individualism in Three Chinese Societies" (Ph.D. diss., Boston University, 1994), p. 127; Hamilton, "Culture and Organization," pp. 47–48. The relative immunity of Taiwan from the Asian financial crisis of 1997–1998 also relates to the size and strength of this petty entrepreneurial economy, compared to Korea or Indonesia.

20. Much of this material is based on interviews with forty-three entrepreneurs (including twenty-one women) conducted in Tianjin, Chongqing, and Hainan during the summer of 1993 by Jiansheng Li and Zhang Yuehong, under my direction. This work was funded by the Institute for the Study of Economic Culture at Boston University.

21. Jiansheng Li, "Changing Kinship Relations and Their Effects on Contemporary Urban Chinese Society" (Ph.D. diss., Boston University, 1999).

22. This has been documented in Li, "Changing Kinship."

23. See McEwen, "Markets, Modernization, and Individualism," ch. 3, p. 320.

24. Yan, *The Flow of Gifts*, p. 77.

25. Wank, "Private Business, Bureaucracy, and Political Alliance in a Chinese City."

26. See Terry Sicular, "Redefining State, Plan and Market: China's Reforms in Agricultural Commerce," in Andrew G. Walder, ed., *China's Transitional Economy* (New York: Oxford University Press, 1996), pp. 58–84, on the blurring of the line between market and plan.

27. We know, in addition, that all kinds of personal ties play important roles in Western business, and researchers have not yet attempted a systematic comparison that might reveal just how different the use of connections really is between China and the West in practice.

28. See, for example, Thomas B. Gold, "After Comradeship: Personal Relations in China Since the Cultural Revolution," *China Quarterly* 104 (December 1985), pp. 657–675.

29. The ambivalence toward kinship is clear in our own interviews, and in Susan McEwen's, "Markets, Modernization, and Individualism in Three Chinese Societies" (pp. 140–144, 240, 305–306), a study of entrepreneurs in Taiwan, Hong Kong, and Guangzhou.

30. Early wage labor opportunities for women in the late nineteenth and early twentieth centuries opened up a few opportunities for women to escape this system, but in general their production continued to remain tied to the household and controlled by men. See Topley, "Marriage Resistance in Rural Kwangtung," in Wolf and Witke, eds., *Women in Chinese Society*; and Lynda S. Bell, "For Better, for Worse: Women and the World Market in Rural China," *Modern China* 20(2) (1994), pp. 180–210.

31. While the theory was clear, the practice varied widely. Strong lineages in fact kept affines off the main ancestral altar under all circumstances, but poor areas with weak or no lineages often welcomed any ties they could get, and one could easily find villages where altars with tablets of three or four different surnames were not unusual. See Weller, *Unities and Diversities*, p. 31.

32. Wolf, *Women and the Family in Rural Taiwan*, pp. 32–41.

33. McEwen, "Markets, Modernization, and Individualism," pp. 231–232.

34. Kellee S. Tsai, "A Circle of Friends, a Web of Trouble: Rotating Credit Associations in China," *Harvard China Review* 1(1) (1998), p. 82.

35. Tsai ("A Circle of Friends," p. 83) shows how rotating credit associations in Wenzhou developed into something like pyramid schemes (and collapsed like pyramid schemes) when they moved beyond the realm of face-to-face trust in the 1980s.

36. McEwen, "Markets, Modernization, and Individualism," p. 340.

37. Only two of the nineteen had been in business for more than five years, and seven for less than one year. Twelve were over the age of thirty-five.

38. McEwen, "Markets, Modernization, and Individualism," pp. 162, 254.

39. Hill Gates, "'Narrow Hearts' and Petty Capitalism: Small Business Women in Chengdu, China," in Alice Littlefield and Hill Gates, eds., *Marxist Approaches in Economic Anthropology* (Lanham, Md.: University Press of America, 1991), p. 25. See also McEwen, "Markets, Modernization, and Individualism," p. 346.

40. See also McEwen, "Markets, Modernization, and Individualism," 1994, pp. 148, 239, 341–342.

41. This attitude is apparently widespread among both women and men. Many people interviewed in 1993 showed it, and Mayfair Mei-hui Yang documents the same thing in *Gifts, Favors and Banquets*, p. 83.

42. McEwen, "Markets, Modernization, and Individualism," p. 244.

43. Unofficially, about half of Taiwan's corporate assets may have been controlled directly or indirectly by the state and Party in 1990, see Hsiao, "The State and Business Relations in Taiwan," p. 5.

44. Ibid., p. 86.

45. Tien Hung-mao and Cheng Tun-jen, "Crafting Democratic Institutions in Taiwan," *China Journal* 37 (1997), p. 24.

46. Christopher Earle Nevitt, "Private Business Associations in China: Evidence of Civil Society or State Power?" *China Journal* 36 (1996), pp. 25–43; Jonathan Unger, "'Bridges': Private Business, the Chinese Government and the Rise of New Associations," *China Quarterly* 147 (1996), pp. 795–819; and Wank, "Private Business."

47. Unger, "Bridges," p. 812.

48. Wank, "Private Business."

49. Kelliher, *Peasant Power in China.*

50. Field notes of Zhang Yuehong, Chongqing, 1993, as part of this project.

51. Redding, "'Thickening' Civil Society."

52. On the stock market, see Ellen Hertz, *The Trading Crowd: An Ethnography of the Shanghai Stock Market* (Cambridge, Mass.: Cambridge University Press, 1998). She argues that in spite of continued government manipulation and a general lack of transparency, the volatile Shanghai market of 1992 taught regulators that there were limits on what they could control.

53. Tienand Cheng, "Crafting Democratic Institutions in Taiwan," p. 24.

5

Religion: Local Association and Split Market Cultures

At first glance local Chinese temple religion appears to offer the kind of intermediate social organization between the private family and the public state that much recent literature on civil society has emphasized. Temples define social boundaries in ritual, organize neighborhoods to provide support, offer points of contact for local leaders, and provide public symbols of community. Yet if we look more closely, these temple communities are rather different from the kinds of civil association that the literature on Europe has emphasized. Unlike theoretical descriptions of the European case, Chinese temple communities are not strictly voluntary because they are built primarily around communal ties of geography, not individual choice. As I will discuss, their loyalties are also fundamentally localist, posing natural problems for any development into a base for national civil association. The first goal of this chapter is to spell out the ways in which such groups still contribute an independent voice of a local public sphere—perhaps not a civil society, but an alternative vehicle for social capital and political transformation.

The second goal is to complicate this picture by showing how religion has evolved under the different modernities of Taiwan and China, creating still further permutations of civil association. As in many parts of the world, Taiwan and China have stymied the old predictions that market modernity would lead to an inevitable secularization. There may be more religious activity in Taiwan now than ever in the past, and religion has been growing rapidly in China since the end of the powerful repression of the Cultural Revolution period. In part this involves a revival and retrenchment of old forms, but two other developments particularly stand out. First is an increase in the aspects of worship that are most individualistic, least communitarian, and least committed to public morality—

neither very civil nor very social. Second, however, is change in just the opposite direction: an increase in organized, universalizing religions that seem more familiar to those searching for equivalents to Western civil society. These are voluntary congregations of people with common beliefs, including Christianity (primarily in China), but more importantly new Buddhist movements and outgrowths of earlier sectarian groups. These two kinds of religious changes seem at odds with each other—one ignoring traditional moralities and the other preaching them at length, one ephemeral and the other based in lasting congregations. Their simultaneous development, I will argue, shows the sort of split culture that typifies an emergent market logic. It appears both to strip off old conventions, allowing a consumption unfettered by custom, and to call out for new communities and new moralities. Each of these possibilities has quite different implications for political change, and I will return to this problem at the end of this chapter.

Local Temple Religion

Temples are built above all on geographical communities.[1] Earth god (*tudi gong*) worship in many parts of China, for example, rotates among all the households in a neighborhood. Moving to a new neighborhood means making offerings to a new earth god. Larger temples also clearly mark their territories, especially when gods tour their realms in sedan chairs. Still larger communities may be defined through "incense division" (*fenxiang*), when a new temple buds off from an old one by taking some of its incense ash. These larger communities may no longer be geographically united, but still share close economic and migration ties. Even very successful community temples rarely had ties extending as far as the provincial level, although their deities could be worshipped more broadly through other temple networks. Most temples have an authority that stops at the level of their town and surrounding villages.

The community itself funds and controls these temples. Priests will be brought in to perform rituals, but actual management falls to local secular leaders organized in a committee like other traditional Chinese corporations. This is thus a particularly amorphous sort of religion, where local temples rest almost entirely on an independent social base with essentially no larger institutions of control. Being a member of a community means worshipping at certain temples for most people in Taiwan and Hong Kong, and increasingly again in parts of the People's Republic. While there is a voluntary element—no one is compelled to worship any particular god—the primary identification of a worshiper is communal.

One can see this also in the actions of gods. The deity I know best, Qingshui Zushi Gong at his temple in the Taiwanese town of Sanxia, was famous for helping people in his community while ignoring others. When Taiwanese soldiers were drafted by the Japanese to fight in southeast Asia during World War II, for example, Zushi Gong was said to have warned several Sanxia natives of impending bombing raids, while leaving other Taiwanese soldiers to their fates. Although some gods have acted in the national interest and thus been recognized by the imperial state, even they are mostly known locally for local actions.[2]

Financially these temples are also creations of local community. Money comes from a combination of voluntary donations and, for some rituals, the equivalent of a household tax. The Sanxia temple to Qingshui Zushi Gong, for example, raised money for its annual ritual to appease the lonely ghosts by assigning village heads—elected government officials—to collect a fee from every household in their village.

This kind of interpenetration with local politics was not uncommon. Like many community temples in Taiwan, this one served as the base for one of the local political factions, whose members were well represented on the temple committee. With no legal opposition parties before martial law was lifted in Taiwan, temples provided one of the only reliable bases of community organization. Temples like these continue to be among the clearest symbols of local identity and among the only community-wide social organizations outside the government. This is surely part of the reason they have continued to thrive in the last few decades.

We know much less about temple religion currently in the People's Republic of China, but it is possible to estimate some of the patterns in its recreation.[3] This kind of religion was passively discouraged after 1949, and very actively attacked during the Cultural Revolution, essentially ending all public religious activity until the late 1970s. Even in the Cultural Revolution the repression of religion was not thorough, as many people practiced in secret, or hid away religious images and texts. With the increased personal freedoms of the 1980s and 1990s, many of these objects and rituals returned to the public eye, and temples and their communities began to be rebuilt in parts of China.

The current evidence suggests that the recreation of temple religion is taking place differently across China, and that this in part reflects differences in the strength and nature of the informal social sector. First, there are more new or rebuilt local temples in the southeastern provinces of Fujian, Guangdong and Guangxi than one sees north of the Yangzi River. The differences may in part represent prerevolutionary variations in religious culture. They clearly also reflect the more rapid economic development of the southeast in recent years, and a greater distance from the political control of the center. There is simply more room for an informal political center in the south, where a richer private economy allows investment in local religion, and a more distant central government allows more free space for such activities. Rapid rebuilding of community temples also clearly correlates with close ties to overseas communities. These communities will frequently contribute large amounts of money toward reconstruction of temples, and local communities often hope and expect that this will ease other kinds of investment. Local governments allow more leeway in these cases because keeping good economic ties with overseas communities is important to them.[4] Even when this is true, however, these temples are again organizing their own local communities by raising money and putting on joint public rituals. In the process they are again establishing local community networks through an organization between family and state. The result is a distinct pattern in China, where many temples are now easily visible in the rural southeast, but very few, for example, in the northeast.[5]

Second, there are more temples in rural areas than urban. Again this may tie to the relatively tighter political control in urban areas. In addition, the dominance of the state-owned economic sector in urban areas creates a much stronger official organization of social life through work units, leaving less room for temples to develop. Outside of state enterprise units, especially in areas with a large "floating" population, cities lack the strong sense of community that villages retain.

Third, grave cleaning and other rituals associated with ancestors have revived more quickly and universally than temple rituals. The explanation probably again lies in the amount of free space left open for religious activities of various types. Ancestral rituals are important primarily at the level of families rather than intermediate civil or community groups. Large lineage rituals, which involve larger groups of people, have been much slower to come back. In part, veneration of ancestors is so intimately tied to Chinese images of their own culture that it is more difficult for the state to oppose. This is one reason public demonstrations sometimes safely take the form of funerals (most notably for Zhou Enlai and later Hu Yaobang) when other forms would not be permitted.[6] Temples and their rituals, however, are more easily branded as superstition. They also involve larger communities of people and therefore more easily draw the gaze of the local authorities. It is simply riskier to build a temple than to sweep a grave, and so people have been slower to do it.[7]

Fourth, shamanic practices and spirit possession appear to be widespread, if not entirely above ground, in many parts of rural China, even where community temples have not been rebuilt. I found this to be the case in eastern Guangxi province during the mid-1980s, and there are similar reports from Gansu, far to the northwest. Many of these spirit mediums now are women, almost surely more than before the Revolution. This also relates to the free space the state leaves for religion, and I will take it up again below in the section on women and religion.

Finally, very small temples like earth god shrines (*tudi miao, shetan*) have been rebuilt before larger community temples.[8] Small shrines are cheaper to build, of course. They are also less visible than larger temples, and thus less likely to attract unwelcome attention. Perhaps most importantly, these are the temples with the most intimate ties to local settlements (natural villages, roughly equivalent to the earlier production teams). This is the most vibrant community level, the one with the strongest cohesion under the current economic and political system.

Taken together, these scraps of evidence contribute to a picture of an informal political sector with a significant local religious component in parts of China. The variations also show how important the government is in defining space for public association. Religion thrives especially where the central bureaucrats are more distant—the south, rural areas, and at small scales. Given the opportunity, temples and community rituals like god processions are again helping to create and define communities in much of China. They form part of the internal structure of communities, and in some cases also part of the external connections among communities. They draw people together as part of a recreation of community and individual identity. Even when the local government looks on benignly, they also imply a kind of gentle political criticism of a state that clearly disapproves.

This played out clearly in Anxi county, Fujian, when it tried to revive the annual rituals for the birthday of their major community god in 1986 and 1987.[9] They had begun with secret nighttime festivities in 1984, and then added some monks and more open parades in 1985. Encouraged by this, they decided to operate on a much larger scale in 1986, with significant funding coming from overseas Chinese. This time, however, authorities felt things had gone too far, and stepped in with the police to arrest and fine Daoists and other key participants. At some points the crowds actively impeded the police, allowing one prisoner to escape, and the police could not stop the festival from carrying out its agenda. Police interference was further minimized in 1987, when local political leaders interceded with higher-level officials, arguing successfully that the overseas donors were unhappy. Mixed in with this conflict were still other efforts by smaller communities within the county to assert their own power against each other, and the moments of transition from one group carrying the god through its territory to the next group were often very tense. These kinds of tensions are not simply about the state versus society; they are instead about the competing interests of local societies, complicated by the government's frowning on "superstition" while welcoming overseas cash in any form.

Yet, as in Taiwan, this is not an Enlightenment sort of civil society.[10] These temples are fundamentally localist and communitarian in orienta-

tion, with little historical or comparative reason to think they will develop into forces at the level of the whole nation. In addition, as with
other kinds of intermediate social groups, the Chinese government will
not allow enough free space for the development of independent religious associations as part of a civil society. It either represses them (as
with independent labor unions, for example), or co-opts them into corporatist organizations that it controls (like many business associations).
The Daoist Association and religious bureaucracy are attempts to control
religion; occasional clampdowns on "superstition" or religious "charla-
tans," or forbidding temples from doing large public rituals of renewal
(*jiao*) are attempts to repress. The state has eased up greatly on religion
over the last decade, yet any larger kind of growth is clearly out of the
question under the current regime. Temple religion will remain localist
and communitarian, but it also remains an important point of concentration for social capital. Taiwan clearly shows the potential importance of
this for political change when temples help organize secular social movements (as I will discuss in the next chapter) and when politicians feel
compelled to seek their support.

New Selves and New Moralities

The consolidation and recreation of local community temples in Taiwan
and China is far from the whole story. Both places have also seen the
rapid growth of religious alternatives, often based on resources that were
already there, but also often evolving in new ways. These include increased interest in ghost worship (primarily in Taiwan), spirit mediums,
pietistic sects based in earlier Chinese movements like the White Lotus,
new Buddhist organizations, and Christianity and Islam (primarily in
China, not Taiwan). One set of these—including the spirit mediums and
the ghosts—tends toward utilitarian granting of individual desires, dissolving the local community interests of temple-based religion. The other
set looks instead to universalizing sets of moral values, defining new
kinds of communities no longer based on local geography. Only this second set constitutes anything like a civil association, but I will consider
both here because they constitute two sides of a single phenomenon—
they are the split cultural response to a rapidly expanding market economy.

The idea that market modernity would encourage religious development may seem counterintuitive. Most of the founders of modern social
thought—Marx and Weber above all—expected an ultimate secularization under capitalism. These expectations dominated social science
through the 1960s, but simply have not stood the empirical test of time.
With the arguable exception of Western Europe, religion has thrived

around the world in the twentieth century. These analysts were correct that the pressures of a market economy would encourage powerful social changes, including challenges to earlier kinds of community morality. The necessity to maximize profits pressures people to loosen other kinds of ties. At the same time, areas of life that had never been experienced as part of the economic sphere (child care, religion, food preparation) increasingly appear as commodities and become open to the rationalizing disciplines of the market. The result is that market modernity is often also perceived as a crisis of values, as selfishness overwhelms any sense of community.

Yet there is nothing inevitable or unstoppable about this process. It is challenged and compromised at all points by people making sense of their changing world. Capitalism thus did not spell the end of religion, but instead has seen the sorts of religious revivals that have typified nineteenth-century America as much as late twentieth-century Iran. The challenges to a strict market logic come both from compromises with existing social and cultural resources, and from more direct reactions that attempt to reconstruct "lost" moral worlds.

Individualizing Religions

One kind of religious reaction to the perceived crisis of morality in market societies is simply to accept the new individualism and utilitarianism, playing up aspects of the existing religious repertoire that best fit that image. Chinese popular religion has long included a strong individualistic streak, especially through the worship of ghosts.[11] The very definition of ghosts rests on their existence apart from any normal social ties: They are the unincorporated dead, part of no larger social group. One worships ghosts for personal gain, not for family or community. Ghosts work on a contract basis, with quick and nasty punishment for not paying them back on time, and without regard for broader issues of morality. The ghostly marketplace for miracles exchanges cash for services and leaves no lasting personal ties.

Ghosts' individualizing function contrasts with the community base of gods, and their faceless anonymity and insistence on keeping the terms of a bargain recalls the market in ways that political petitions and tribute payments to gods do not. The annual ghost festival repeats the same message when the priests throw coins out to the greedy ghosts and to the spectators struggling for them below. The single sticks of incense in ghost offerings (or single cigarettes in some cases) also emphasize their individuality and lack of community ties, and contrast strongly with the massive piles of incense and combined clouds of smoke in more standard shared incense pots for gods or ancestors. In a society that long had an important market component, it should not surprise us that an individualistic, even selfish undercurrent ran beneath the niceties of bureaucratic hierarchy in god worship and fraternal unity in the ancestor cult.

The ghostly side of Chinese religion in Taiwan (the only area for which we have extensive data so far) grew very rapidly in the 1980s, at the point when many Taiwanese for the first time had achieved some significant wealth, but when the market economy also appeared particularly threatening and capricious, with few productive outlets for capital.[12] A number of ghost temples suddenly became prominent at this time in Taiwan because they would grant any request regardless of morality, in exchange for a material gift to their temple. They were not evil so much as just amoral—market relationships fetishized. The most spectacular of these ghost cults was the shrine to the Eighteen Lords, which became for a few years Taiwan's most popular temple. The Eighteen Lords were seventeen unidentified dead men who floated ashore in northern Taiwan at some forgotten time in the past, most likely victims of a fishing disaster. The eighteenth was a living dog who jumped into the grave of his dead masters and was buried with them. Taiwanese typically build a small shrine when they find unidentified human remains, and this one was particularly unimportant until the 1980s. At that point it became famous for successfully granting all kinds of requests, and was said to be frequented especially by prostitutes, gangsters, gamblers, and above all people trying to get winning numbers in an illegal lottery.[13] They would do anything at all in exchange for payment, and granted requests that gods in community temples would not consider.

Another major religious growth area in both China and Taiwan has been spirit medium cults. These are usually based in private altars as a kind of small business. Like the ghosts, they provide utilitarian help to individuals representing their own (or their immediate family's) interests with none of the communal functions of major temples. As usual, we know more about the situation in Taiwan, which has seen a great increase in these cults. At the same time, more and more different gods are appearing on these private altars. Community temples usually feature one primary deity, often captured in many images. Other gods may appear on secondary altars, or in minor positions on the main altar. The horde of different gods on private spirit medium altars—as many as forty or fifty different images in recent years—reinforces the utilitarian functions of such cults.[14] With each deity having its own specialty, these temples can meet the needs of a wider variety of clients, just like a shop that expands its selection of wares. Not coincidentally, spirit medium shrines themselves are profit-oriented petty capitalist enterprises.

We do not yet have comparable data from China, but we know of an increase in spirit mediumship in a number of areas, even in the absence of a resurgence of temple-based religion. In rural Guangxi in 1985, for example, villages were just starting to build earth god shrines, and larger community temples had not yet come back. Spirit mediums were widespread, though. As in Taiwan, these mediums provide a service for which one pays cash. In two instances I had local officials tell me about uncanny experiences they had had with mediums, even as they explained that they were good Communists and educated men, and did not believe in superstition. In one case the medium cured an illness, and in the other found the lost grave of an ancestor.[15] The individualizing effects of this kind of market-based religion echo in other religious developments in China. Helen Siu shows how ritual has become increasingly utilitarian and less tied to old community and kinship moralities as it has revived in part of rural Guangdong.[16] None of this is quite as startling as Taiwan's massive crowds and carnival atmosphere at the Eighteen Lords temple, but it also reflects a growing individualistic and utilitarian streak in a religion increasingly characterized by monetary relationships.

Moralizing Religions

The process I have been discussing recalls arguments in the West about the modern decline of associational life—ghost worship is the Taiwanese equivalent of bowling alone. Yet while its rise clearly correlates with growing market economies in China and Taiwan, it is not the only important religious response. These individualizing bits of religion are met by other movements that are deeply dissatisfied with what they perceive as a crisis of morality in the new economy, and that offer substitutes very different from both community temple worship or the newly popular ghost and spirit medium cults. This moralizing side of the split market culture creates voluntary social unities that are far closer to the idea of civil associations.

These new movements are sects in Max Weber's sense that membership is voluntary and individualistic, not simply given by birth or residence. Weber, writing primarily about Protestant denominations in the United States, pointed out that members of the same sect can be trusted because all are like-minded people, having consciously chosen certain kinds of values.[17] Participants in the community temple worship or the more individual activities I have just described, on the other hand, have no such guarantees. Anyone is qualified to worship, and one learns little about someone's values by knowing that they have gone to a community temple. The new religions, however, have exactly the sectarian structure that Weber discussed. Most of my discussion here will be about pietistic sects like the Way of Unity (Yiguan Dao), which grew very rapidly in the 1970s and 1980s. All these pietistic sects have clearly organized congregations, a syncretic and universalizing theology, an active concern for evangelization, and an interest in religious texts with commentaries often produced through spirit writing. The groups I will discuss are now based in Taiwan, although they originated on the mainland and their current situation in China is not at all clear. It is generally not legal to organize such groups there, and while one hears of various sects popping up, it is impossible to gather systematic data. To an extent, however, Christianity and Islam occupy the same niche there.

Taiwanese sectarians, just like Weber's Protestants, substitute a self-selected group of trustworthy (and therefore creditworthy) comrades for the potential problems of ascribed particularistic ties like kinship or residence. Even their vegetarianism, which many of the sects require, marks them as different kinds of individuals, especially at business or religious feasts, which generally feature overflowing platters of meat. Their regular meetings, spirit-writing or spirit-possession sessions, and greater moral discipline distinguish them from the rest of society, and offer them a new kind of social resource in business. Worship of a single primary goddess, which typifies many of these groups, also cuts members off from the local associations of community temples, and furthers their sectarian separation.

These sectarians also heavily emphasize explicit, textually validated values, unlike the pragmatic attitude of most popular religious practice. In particular, they consider themselves to be reviving threatened traditional Chinese values as expressed in Confucian and Daoist classics.[18] Many spirit-writing sessions produce commentaries on classics, and these may be discussed in regular meetings that resemble a combination of Protestant preaching and Sunday school. Several sects also produce magazines or sponsor inspirational speakers to promote their values. Constant themes include conservative standards in Taiwan like filial piety, respect for authority, and keeping appropriate relations of hierarchy between men and women, seniors and juniors, parents and children.[19] This is the other side of the celebration of individual autonomy and self-interest in ghost worship and spirit medium altars: an attempt to retrieve communal values in an era that has lost them. While these sects do embrace a kind of individualism, they embed it firmly in Confucian discourse of broader social relations. They are the spirit-writing equivalent of the philosophers trying to reclaim Confucianism as a moral alternative for the modern world.

The most important of these sects has been the Way of Unity (Yiguan Dao), which controls most of the vegetarian restaurants in Taiwan, and also boasts the active membership of Zhang Rongfa, one of the island's wealthiest businessmen. It claims over a million followers (almost 5 percent of the island's population).[20] Many of the sects claim strong business support, and anecdotal evidence suggests that a disproportionate number of businessmen are sectarians.[21] These assertions have not been proven, but they certainly recall the claim that Protestant sects offer a set of like-minded moral associates and thus potential business connections.[22] In some cases, all or most of the employees of small factories may be members of the same group as their boss.[23] Membership appears to have grown rapidly just during the period of Taiwan's most rapid economic growth.

I took part in the meeting of a smaller, but similar sect called Raozhi in 1978. It was also run by a small circle of businessmen, and its core group met every three days. When I visited we all donned white robes and sat together for a study session on the divine commentary from the previous session. We then offered incense at the altar and the medium received the next installment of the commentary, part of a continuing explanation of the Daoist classic, the *Daode Jing*. Despite the spirit writing, the feeling was very formal and Confucian—men on the left and women on the right, matching robes, and coordinated movements on cue from the group leader.

These sects provide a very different take on market morality than the ghosts or spirit mediums. Of all the religious phenomena I have discussed, they are most clearly like standard civil associations. Like local community temples (and unlike the ghosts and spirit mediums) they are reservoirs of social capital, which they mobilize in generally conservative political causes and in business ventures. Unlike the more traditional temples, however, they are based on truly voluntary membership that often crosscuts older ties of community and kinship. This gives them the potential to act on a larger scale than other religious groups in Taiwan. Finally, it is worth recalling that in China such groups have their heads cut off, and religion is thus most significant there at a local level only. This is comparable to the situation for business and other kinds of associations, and reminds us again how important the state is in defining the amount of free space open to civil organization.

Women and Religion

One striking characteristic of recent religious developments in both China and Taiwan has been the public role of women. In China this has primarily occurred through the revival of shamanism, which now appears to be dominated by women in a way never before true. In Taiwan the most important case is the Compassionate Relief Merit Society (Ciji Gongdehui), whose membership is about 80 percent women, and which has grown into the largest civil organization in Taiwan. These two cases are very different from each other, but both show the ways that women can turn their difficult social positions into a form of public power through religion.

I will take these two examples up in detail in a moment, but it is worth noting first how much both vary from the more domestic religious role that women usually played in earlier times. Women conducted most of the daily worship of household gods and ancestors across China and Taiwan. The man's role is strongest at only the most formal, public, and important ritual occasions—funerals, *jiao* ceremonies of community and temple renewal (where women are usually forbidden to enter the temple), core functions of large lineages, and similar occasions. Women, however, care for the daily needs of the ancestors, and for most larger household rituals. Yet these are also her husband's ancestors, by whose worship on her wedding day she marked the putative end of her membership in her own natal family.

Chinese popular worship had very few opportunities for roles in larger social organizations. People could join local temple management committees, or take organizing roles in large community rituals. Men dominated all of these positions, however, and none of them offered opportunities beyond the local community. Popular worship had little for women dissatisfied with their role at home.

There were a few other religious options open to some women. The most radical was monastic Buddhism. Women always had the option of "leaving the family" (*chujia*) to become nuns, striving for perfection by leaving the secular world and its trappings of meat, hair, and desire. Yet this also always posed problems for women. Just the phrase "leaving the family" implies the greatest criticism of monastic Buddhism in China: its fundamental breach of filial piety, which requires bearing sons as much as caring for parents. Duty to family discouraged most women from this path at least as much as the rigorous disciplines of the monastery. In modern China and Taiwan, this option suffers from the further critique that it flees from real problems; it is irrelevant to the worlds of these women.

Becoming a nun was never an important option to the majority of women, but they could more plausibly consider joining lay Buddhist groups that centered around the singing of sutras. Many of these meet in community temples or in their own "vegetarian halls" (*zhai tang*), and were very popular in Taiwan and elsewhere.[24] They offer women a world of their own, where they can take on organizing roles, and where they can develop a Buddhist religiosity without leaving the family. They sing together, sometimes without understanding the words of the sutras. People also sometimes hire these groups to recite sutras, especially for funeral services.

Lay Buddhist groups offered women room for self-cultivation without the moral and personal dilemmas of becoming a nun. Their role in funerals and other services also created a small independent income. More importantly for most women, they also created a sense of accomplishment in a more public sphere to which they normally had little access. The epitome of such things were the women's houses in some silk-producing districts of Guangdong in the nineteenth century. In these cases women used their silk-factory income to escape from marriage, living together as a lay Buddhist community.[25] Still, such organizations existed only on a very modest scale, even in the extreme Guangdong case. The more typical groups had strong ties to local temples and lacked any centralized organization, leaving them inherently parochial. They were the closest thing to a formal civil association of women, but still had only a limited public role.

Women Spirit Mediums

Spirit mediumship took different forms across China and Taiwan, but it was widespread in late imperial times. These mediums have clients rather than congregations, but regular patrons will often gather together for sessions at the medium's altar, forming a kind of informal network.[26] The clients usually want illnesses cured or bad luck changed. In its most common form a deity—usually not an important local community god—will possess the medium's body to diagnose the problem and perhaps write a curing charm. While such performances can be dramatic, with the medium taking on the personality of the god, they also have a mundane quality where one simply converses with the deity. None of China's twentieth-century governments has been especially happy about the practice. Republican or Communist, spirit mediums offended their modernist sensibilities. Campaigns against it in both Taiwan and China usually reduced mediums to simple frauds who extorted money from their superstition-ridden victims.[27] The extent of the campaigns, however, also shows how difficult it was to end such practices. Taiwan never succeeded in stopping the practice, and it is now extremely widespread.

Given the far more powerful repression of these practices in the People's Republic, especially during the Cultural Revolution, their widespread resurgence appears even more remarkable.[28] In most parts of China the medium could traditionally be male or female, but women dominate the new pattern.[29] Jun Jing describes twenty-three mediums in northwest China, all women who practice curing.[30] While he heard of a few male mediums, the vast majority are now female there, and this is quite different from the more balanced pattern before 1949. The earliest of these women had begun to practice at a makeshift shrine as early as 1975, during the waning years of the Cultural Revolution.

Why women? One of Jing's informants summed up his explanation: "Women could go there to burn incense under the sunlight. Men could

go there to kowtow only under the moonlight. The world was turned up-
side down."[31] That is, even under the current period of relative relaxation
about religion, most men in most of China feel they have too much to
lose by taking part in such activity. Women's behavior, however, is taken
less seriously by the androcentric political system. In addition, the
women involved generally have already raised their children. With most
of their social responsibilities achieved, they feel they have little to lose.
Here is a case where women are able to play on their marginal position
in the political and social hierarchy to achieve another kind of power.
Spirit mediumship creates this possibility for women in many societies.[32]
It is especially interesting in China, where this development has put
women at the forefront of the religious resurgence, and allowed them to
create a new medium for local informal ties.

A very similar case can be made for northern Vietnam, again where
women were both looked down upon and largely overlooked by local
political authorities, and where a little free space for religion has begun to
open up after a period of powerful repression.[33] As in China, women
have led a resurgence of spirit mediumship. Most remarkable, however,
has been women's participation in village communal house rituals, an
arena from which they had been banned completely in prerevolutionary
days. This radical revision of earlier ritual at women's hands was again
possible because of the greater political liabilities of men.

In the area of religion, at least, these cases suggest that women play a
pivotal role in the creation of new kinds of local social networks outside
the state, seeing and occupying areas of free space that are not available
to men. This is reminiscent of women's more active roles in rotating
credit associations, which I mentioned in the previous chapter. The combination of gender bias and authoritarian politics puts these women at
the forefront of developing a social world apart from the state, an informal civil world. If this is true, it also suggests that men may follow in
their footsteps, perhaps ultimately displacing them in part, if things continue to loosen up. This has begun to happen in northern Vietnam, where
men in some villages began to recapture their communal ceremonies
after a few years, and may be happening in the parts of China with the
most active public religion, like southern Fujian.[34]

Women and Taiwanese Buddhism

The most striking of all the recent religious changes in Taiwan has been
the rebirth of Buddhism in the form of huge lay associations with monastic leadership. Each of the largest organizations has millions of followers
whose contributions have created enormous coffers. These groups typically take on major social functions in addition to their religious ones.

The most important activities are secular education, welfare, and in some cases politics.[35] The largest and wealthiest is the Compassionate Relief Merit Society (Ciji Gongdehui), which claimed almost 4 million members (perhaps 20 percent of the population), and gave away more than US$ 20 million each year in charitable aid in 1991.[36] It runs a major hospital in Taiwan, conducts a welfare operation that rivals the Taipei city government, and now has branches all over the world. A charismatic Buddhist nun named Zhengyan founded the organization in the 1960s on Taiwan's poor eastern coast. Her handful of lay followers contributed daily pin money and sold handicrafts to fund charity for the ill.

The organization really boomed, however, with the economic growth and political loosening of the 1980s. Many members now contribute as much as NT$1 million (about US$40,000) annually. In addition to their sheer size, the most striking feature of the group is its gender balance— the members are about 80 percent women.[37] A core membership of several thousand (again 70 to 80 percent female) carries the main weight, giving large donations, soliciting new members, and identifying needy families.

Many of the followers who flocked to the movement in the last decade are only "checkbook members," whose commitment does not extend beyond monthly contributions. Yet Zhengyan has never been satisfied with that, and a large core of the movement consists of people who commit much of their time to organization activities, and who draw others in. Movement literature constantly promotes pragmatic activities over financial contributions. These activities range from changing the habits of daily life (members should not drink or smoke, avoid makeup and fancy clothes, and wear their seat belts) to physically bringing food to the poor or sorting out recycled trash. Many women, some of them quite wealthy, undergo a long waiting list to volunteer for brief stints as candy stripers at the hospital.

In addition to their charitable duties, local Compassionate Relief groups meet regularly. Core members may chant a sutra together and there are study groups to discuss how Zhengyan's writings (especially *Still Thoughts by Dharma Master Zhengyan*) relate to the problems of daily life.[38] The discussion always turns on concrete action rather than Buddhist philosophy, ritual, and text. The testimonials usually either retrace the speaker's path from misery to happiness through joining the group, or confess continuing inadequacies. The constant theme throughout is the remaking of individuals' lives through charity, and the striving of all to reach a kind of perfection that can never be realized (except perhaps by the Master herself).

Local offices are organized by county and city, with district leaders appointed from the central organization mainly based on seniority. At the most local level small groups organize activities in the community. Local members, for example, will identify deserving poor in their areas, or directly deliver aid to needy households. Others organize recycling drives or pursue other environmental activities.[39] These local groups have freedom to pursue their own ends within the guidelines set by the broader organization. Foreign branches work in much the same ways.

Many of the followers' stories speak of alcoholic husbands, shrewish mothers-in-law, and disappointing children. Compassionate Relief teaches them to accept their problems, gives them a supportive group of friends, and offers new interests that give them a feeling of worthy accomplishment. It defuses the domestic problems inherent in being a Chinese wife and mother by reducing them to karma or fate (*yuan*), and offering charitable action as the way to improve karma.

Compassionate Relief focuses action on this world, allowing everyone to act as a bodhisattva. In essence, it urges middle-class women to extend their family values and roles to the wider society, and to forge a new identity as mother to the world. As one member said, "I realized that I used to love too narrowly. I had only two children, whom I was killing with my possessive love. And I was never happy with this aching love. But now I have so many children. I see everyone I help as my own child. I have learned that we have to make our mother love into a world love. And we will live a *practical* life every day! We will be happy every day!"

Another woman expressed very similar sentiments: "My life was too narrow. I lived like a flower in a greenhouse, like a frog in a well. I never knew what the outside world was. Even though I might be a queen at home, what use was it? I told myself, I have to walk out from this small world."

This combination of an emphasis on action over philosophy, an extension of maternal love beyond the family, and support for dealing gently with problems at home has been one of the keys to Compassionate Relief's particular appeal to women. It succeeded only in the 1980s because, in part, it was then that large numbers of women began to have the time and money to put into such an activity, and in part because a booming market modernity sharpened these problems for women at just that time.

Compassionate Relief's unique appeal to women in Taiwan thus stems from its universalization of women's family concerns. It confirms women in their family roles, yet also extends them beyond the family itself for the first time. Unlike many jobs or other public positions, which many women complain bring them into an inappropriate commerce with strangers, this group succeeds in combining a very traditional idea of womanhood with a very modern sphere of action in the world. The wealthy women who form the core membership often feel unfulfilled by their family life. Servants care for the children, and their husbands are busy cultivating business connections, but the women do not want to compromise their roles by entering the economic sphere directly themselves. Many Taiwanese women still speak of the importance of "simplicity," as opposed to the "complexity" of the business world. Compassionate Relief addresses all these issues at once for them.

Both Compassionate Relief and the pietistic sects can be seen as reactions to the perceived loss of communal values with modernity. Beginning with the laments of the Eternal Venerable Mother (Wusheng Laomu, the primary deity for most of them) about the deteriorated state of the world, the pietistic sects continually regret a loss of shared community values (based in Confucianized ideas of filial piety, loyalty, and benevolence) to a grasping individualism. Their language is rather different from Compassionate Relief's, but both see a dangerous lack of morality in the world, and both offer people ways to live their lives in accordance with higher sets of values. As in much of the modernizing world, people fear that shared morality has become greed and selfishness; they feel alienated from an increasingly bureaucratic existence, frustrated at the decay of old social institutions, and lost in the pluralization of everyday life and values.[40]

Yet the differential appeal of Compassionate Relief to wealthy women lies in its differences from these other kinds of movements. The sects have very little to say about charity or a broader caring for the world. Their morality is instead more traditionally Confucian, urging people to act as filial children, and as moral exemplars in their dealings with others. The pietistic sects thus reiterate the old (male-dominated) ideals of Chinese morality, and do not emulate Compassionate Relief's thrust of women's concerns with nurturance onto the world stage. In addition, the sects are much more self-consciously philosophical. For Compassionate Relief, only action counts in the last analysis. Core texts, insofar as they can be said to exist, tend to be stories about real behavior. For the sects, on the other hand, the core texts are commentaries on Confucian classics, written by various deities through the hands of their mediums. Partly for these reasons, the ratio of women to men in Compassionate Relief is far higher than for the sects. They also avoid the sects' enthusiasm for business. Compassionate Relief discourages conspicuous consumption and encourages charity—a nonmarket form of distribution.

Compassionate Relief is currently the largest civil organization in Taiwan, and was the first Buddhist organization recognized as a legal individual (*faren*) since 1950. Its dynamic growth throughout the 1980s led the boom in civil organizations of all kinds in Taiwan during that decade, especially after martial law was lifted in 1987. The Taiwanese government in fact is not at all displeased with this group, whose welfare activities fill an important gap. The late President Jiang Jingguo visited the headquarters as early as 1980, the government has offered some support for the hospital and the medical school, and the foreign ministry likes to take visiting dignitaries to meet Zhengyan. With Taiwan's recent democratization, their massive membership base is also an irresistible target for politicians of all kinds.

Yet Zhengyan and her organization adamantly refuse explicit political activities or endorsements of any kind. Men in the Compassion-Honor Group (Cicheng Dui, a kind of men's auxiliary to the commissioners, founded in 1990) must swear not to participate in politics, as well as to avoid alcohol and to follow other proscriptions. All members were forbidden from campaigning during the 1996 presidential election. While Compassionate Relief has never directly challenged government policy, it has taken its own course, often disappointing politicians of all stripes. Zhengyan herself preaches almost exclusively in Hokkien dialect, although she speaks Mandarin. The public use of Hokkien has been officially frowned upon until recently, and could be taken as support for independence in Taiwan. I have even heard her berate a wheelchair-bound supplicant for speaking Mandarin. On the other hand, the group's gifts of aid to mainland disaster victims have been criticized by pro-independence factions.

Compassionate Relief is a classic civil organization in the sense that it is an intermediate institution between the private world and the state, with a voluntary membership, existing in a legal framework that clearly separates social and state organizations. It is insistently apolitical, yet politically vital as a central field for the redefinition of self and morality.

Split Market Cultures and Civil Association

People in market-based societies feel a push toward increasing commodification and utilitarian exploitation of resources—human, natural, and divine. On the other hand, they also develop strong reactions against a perceived deterioration of shared community and family moralities. While this tension is sometimes phrased as an argument between market and antimarket moralities, it may be better viewed as a split market culture. Both sides of the argument have roots in tradition, just as both sides are in some ways reflexes of the market itself. Thus Confucianism reworked through the divine texts of the Way of Unity offers itself simultaneously as the key to capitalist success and as the answer to the resulting moral vacuum. While ghosts and some spirit mediums cater to individuals and private profit in China and Taiwan, gods and bodhisattvas offer instead community and universal moral worlds. All of them are thriving at once.

The various facets of this split market culture have different implications for the sorts of civil organizations that can serve as reservoirs of social capital—some dissolve them as others build them up again in new ways. The extremely individualistic and utilitarian pole—in this case the Taiwanese ghost cults—recognizes and even celebrates the dissipation of such ties. People worship as individuals, for personal gain, and flagrantly without regard for any communal moralities. They do not even recognize such moralities enough to resist them; they just ignore them, openly and happily.

The spirit mediums share some of the same features. They speed the conversion of religion to a fee-for-service commodity, and cater to personal interests without the public community support of temple religion. In practice, however, they also tend to unite regular groups of clients who socialize around an altar and sometimes clearly do enforce community norms. The scale is small and local, but they do create a kind of community.

Temple-based local religion begins to approach the other end of the scale, with its roots firmly in communities. As always with this form of Chinese religion, however, it is very difficult to build national structures of association. The limitations come from several sources: the close association between particular gods, temples, and localities; the social basis in ties of community rather than some more overarching loyalty; the modernist intentions of all twentieth-century Chinese states, causing elites to back away from what they view as "superstition" (as when both the government and environmental NGOs bemoan the role of religion in local environmental protest); and corporatist states that will simply not allow associations to develop into a self-organized civil sector on a large scale. And yet, for all that, local temple religion is an important intermediate institution, a vital part of many communities in large sections of China. In Taiwan, it has sometimes been an important political force as well, and has realized some of its potential to contribute to new social movements and other signs of a civil society.

Finally, organizations like the Way of Unity or the Compassionate Relief Merit Society are creating new kinds of community on national and even global scales. These groups create congregations of believers who share a set of universalistic values. In that sense these sects are more like Christianity or Islam than neighborhood-based forms of religion. Having cut their ties to local communities, these groups can organize on an international scale. Many of them have taken on functions that go well beyond religion. Compassionate Relief's dedication to medical and welfare issues is the most striking case, but by no means the only one.

Men have dominated (but not monopolized) the post-Confucian philosophizing that seeks moral principles for the modern world in Chinese tradition, just as they dominate many of the new religious sects in Taiwan. Women's voices tend to be less organized, as one might expect from their social position. When they do speak, however, either in individual interviews or through the few organizations they dominate, they often emphasize different points of view from the men. Women speak most strongly about the contradictions between work and family values, about the ideals of nurture (through motherhood or through the bodhisattva ideal), and about extending family values to the society at large. Men's family discourse often turns instead to hierarchies of respect and responsibility, to particularistic duties to the ancestral line, and to creating a patrimony for descendants. Men also dominate the theoretical arena, only to be challenged by the worldly activism of the women's groups.

Like many reactions to the perceived loss of morality in market culture, much of these women's discourse is simultaneously traditional and innovative. In all versions, it draws on conservative ideas of women's strength as care providers, most able to nurture helpless babies into responsible adults. Yet the extension of this idea outside the walls of the home is a crucial innovation, breaking boundaries that have kept women outside the public arena, and opening up a new world for them. It reacts against the promarket strain of market culture, but also fits neatly with the new economic opportunities that women have. In China, where political pressure leaves little space for a truly independent associational life, women's positions let them take the organizational lead.

Notes

1. I am speaking here primarily of the nameless popular worship that characterizes most of China. Buddhist temples associated with clergy have much looser ties to local communities, as I have discussed elsewhere (Weller, *Unities and Diversities,* pp. 110–113). Major pilgrimage sites also represent nongeographic communities, and are often found in geographically marginal areas like mountain tops (see Naquin and Yü, eds., *Pilgrims and Sacred Sites*).

2. See Duara, "Superscribing Symbols." Tian Hou is also reinterpreted locally; see Watson, "Standardizing the Gods." Official attempts to rewrite Zushi Gong as a Chinese nationalist hero (fighting for the remnant of the Song Dynasty) also had very little salience for people in Sanxia, who instead only told tales of local and more recent miracles.

3. We know so little partly because China defines this kind of religious practice as superstition, not religion. As a result, Chinese scholars of religion rarely do research on it, and it is a difficult subject for foreigners. There are, however, a few important exceptions, most notably Dean, *Taoist Ritual.*

4. For examples see Dean, *Taoist Ritual,* pp. 113–114, and Helen F. Siu, "Recycling Rituals: Politics and Popular Culture in Contemporary Rural China," in Perry Link, Richard Madsen, and Paul Pickowicz, eds., *Unofficial China: Popular Culture and Thought in the People's Republic* (Boulder: Westview Press, 1989), p. 133.

5. One study cites an average of six temples per village in Fujian's Putian plains, with forty-five days of ritual performances each year. See Kenneth Dean,

"Ritual and Space: Civil Society or Popular Religion?" in Timothy Brook and B. Michael Frolic, eds., *Civil Society in China*, p. 185.

6. See Weller, *Resistance*, pp. 191–194.

7. In southeastern China, where lineages were often powerful, the government branded lineages and their halls as keys of feudal exploitation, and stopped them more actively than community temples. Private ancestor worship, however, has not been discouraged in the same way since the Cultural Revolution ended. For an example, see Siu, "Recycling Rituals."

8. Again, we have little systematic evidence yet on this, but the pattern seemed clear during my travel through rural parts of Fujian and Guangxi in the mid-1980s.

9. This case is from Dean, *Taoist Ritual*, pp. 103–117.

10. See also Dean, "Ritual and Space."

11. See Weller, *Resistance*, pp. 130–142.

12. Ibid., pp. 148–153.

13. I give a much more detailed account of this temple in Weller, *Resistance*, pp. 124–143.

14. Li Yih-yuan, "Taiwan Minjian Zongjiao de Xiandai Qushi: Dui Peter Berger Jiaoshou Dongya Fazhan Wenhua Yinsu Lun de Huiying [The Modern Tendencies of Taiwan's Popular Religion: A Response to Professor Peter Berger's Theory of Cultural Factors in East Asian Development]," *Wenhua de Tuxiang [The Image of Culture]* vol. 2 (Taipei: Chongchen Wenhua, 1992), pp. 117–138.

15. For other cases see Jun Jing, "Female Autonomy and Female Shamans in Northwest China" (paper presented at the annual meeting of the American Anthropological Association, Atlanta, 1994); and Ann S. Anagnost, "Politics and Magic in Contemporary China," *Modern China* 13(1) (1987), pp. 40–61.

16. Siu, "Recycling Rituals."

17. Weber, "The Protestant Sects."

18. See David K. Jordan and Daniel L. Overmyer, *The Flying Phoenix: Aspects of Chinese Sectarianism in Taiwan* (Princeton: Princeton University Press, 1986), pp. 276–280; and Zheng Zhiming, "Youji Lei Luanshu Suo Xianshi zhi Zongjiao Xin Qushi [The New Trend in Religious Worship as Seen From Biographical Travels, Memoirs]," *Bulletin of the Institute of Ethnology, Academia Sinica* 61 (1987), pp. 105–127.

19. See Zheng, "Youji Lei Luanshu," and Qu Haiyuan [Chiu Hei-yuan], "Minjian Xinyang yu Jingji Fazhan [Popular Beliefs and Economic Development]," Report to the Taiwan Provincial Government (n.p.: Taiwan Shengzhengfu Minzhengting, 1989).

20. Official statistics in 1991 listed about 1.5 million members of such sects, but they fail to distinguish sects officially registered as branches of Buddhism or Daoism (Cihui Tang is the most important), or people who still deny membership because Yiguan Dao had been illegal until 1987.

21. Perhaps 90 percent of Taiwan's vegetarian restaurants, for example, are said to be run by sect members (Zhao Dingjun, "Yiguan Dao Caili Shen Bu Ke Ce [The Immeasurable Wealth of the Yiguan Dao]," *Wealth Magazine* 121 (April 1992), p. 131). See also "Shenmi Jiaopai Chongshi Tianri [A Secret Sect Sees the Light of Day Again]," *Yazhou Zhoukan*, 5 August 1990, pp. 28–39.

22. See Weber, "The Protestant Sects."

23. Ian A. Skoggard, *The Indigenous Dynamic in Taiwan's Postwar Development: The Religious and Historical Roots of Entrepreneurship* (Armonk, N.Y.: M. E. Sharpe, 1996), pp. 169–170.

24. See Weller, *Unities and Diversities*, pp. 45–46.

25. For more on these groups see Topley, "Marriage Resistance in Rural Kwangtung"; Bell, "For Better, For Worse"; and Stockard, *Daughters of the Canton Delta*.

26. The spirit writing in the pietistic sects I just discussed is an exception to this more general pattern of mediumship.

27. See, for example, the cases in Anagnost, "Politics and Magic."

28. Again, we lack good data, but we have reports of extensive activity from places as widespread as Fujian, Guangxi, and Gansu. See Dean, *Taoist Ritual*; Baptandier, "The Lady Linshui"; and Jing, "Female Autonomy."

29. The only exception are the mediums who perform in public temple displays in southern Fujian, as documented in Dean's *Taoist Ritual*. The reasons are that this kind of mediumship is public performance, not private curing, and that the regrowth of community religion has gone further in these areas than almost anywhere else in China.

30. Jing, "Female Autonomy."

31. Ibid., p. 4.

32. See Janice Boddy, *Wombs and Alien Spirits: Women, Men, and the Zar Cult in Northern Sudan* (Madison, Wisc.: University of Wisconsin Press, 1989); Ioan M. Lewis, *Ecstatic Religion: An Anthropological Study of Spirit Possession and Shamanism* (Harmondsworth, England: Penguin, 1971).

33. I take this case from Shaun Kingsley Malarney, "Reconstructing the Public Domain: Changing Women's Roles and the Resurgence of Public Ritual in Contemporary Northern Viet Nam" (paper presented to the annual meeting of the American Anthropological Association, Atlanta, 1994).

34. For Vietnam, see Malarney, "Reconstructing the Public Domain," p. 30. For Fujian, see Dean's examples in *Taoist Ritual*, where male mediums perform in front of temples on important occasions. Unlike the other cases I have discussed, however, these do not involve curings.

35. The three largest groups by far are the Compassionate Relief Merit Society (Ciji Gongdehui, which I discuss in detail here), Dharma Drum Mountain (Fagu Shan, which appeals especially to intellectuals), and Buddha Light Mountain (Fuoguang Shan). Buddha Light Mountain has been the most directly political, most infamously in the contributions it made to the Clinton presidential campaign through a branch temple in Los Angeles.

36. See Lu Hwei-syin, "Women's Self-Growth Groups and Empowerment of the 'Uterine Family' in Taiwan," *Bulletin of the Institute of Ethnology, Academia Sinica* 71 (1991), pp. 29–62; Chien-yu Julia Huang and Robert P. Weller, "Merit and Mothering: Women and Social Welfare in Taiwanese Buddhism," *Journal of Asian Studies* 57(2) (1998), pp. 379–396; and Ciji Gongdehui, "Wuyuan Daci Tongti Dabei [Great Beneficence to Known and Unknown, and Boundless Compassion for All]," brochure (n.p.: n.d.).

37. There are still no exact figures on the proportion of women in the group. Lin conducted a survey of the core group of "commissioners." Lin Benxuan, "Zongjiao Yundong de Shehui Jichu—Yi Ciji Gongdehui Wei Lie [The Social Base of a Religious Movement—The Example of the Compassion Merit Society]" (paper presented to the Conference on the Study of Taiwanese Buddhism, National Taiwan University, 1996). In a sample of 500, he had 157 responses, of whom 88.5 percent were women. There may be a gender bias in who chose to respond, but the figure corresponds to Lin's and my impressions based on participant observation.

38. See also Zhang Wei'an, "Fuojiao Ciji Gongde Hui yu Ziyuan Huishou [The Buddhist Compassion Merit Society and Recycling]" (paper presented at the Workshop on Culture, Media and Society in Contemporary Taiwan, Harvard University, 12 June, 1996), p. 11.

39. See Zhang, "Fuojiao Ciji Gongde Hui."

40. Peter Berger, Brigitte Berger, and Hansfried Kellner, *The Homeless Mind: Modernization and Consciousness* (New York: Vintage, 1973), pp. 181–200.

6

Forms of Association and Social Action

Rather than further multiplying examples of associational life, let me turn now to how and when people mobilize these ties in social action. Local efforts at environmental protection provide my primary example: Taiwan's environmental movement has become very powerful and China has grown increasingly concerned with these problems. I will sometimes draw on other kinds of cases, but always with an eye on how people attempt to influence policy from below, and how they can sometimes pressure the political structure itself.

Much of the variation among the business and religious associations I have been discussing falls along two main dimensions that help explain their potentials for social action: a range from formal to informal organization, and from more voluntary to more communal membership criteria. Figure 6.1 summarizes (and simplifies) these with a few examples. The formal/informal dimension distinguishes the sorts of things one might find in a phone book, like the Audubon Society, a labor union, or a bowling league, from the unlisted numbers, perhaps most famously the sort of people Habermas describes hanging out at coffeehouses.[1] To be more precise, I mean something parallel to the differences economists draw between the officially recognized economic system and the informal economy, which includes things like unregistered stalls or forms of credit with no legal support (like rotating credit associations). This informal economy is not necessarily illegal, but simply exists beyond the lines of legitimate activity drawn by the government. Similarly, the informal social sector in the preceding chapters is the part that escapes registration, control, and surveillance by legitimate government power. Those processes of control themselves help generate other features of formality—written rules, official hierarchies, and the rest.

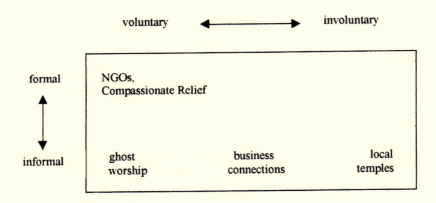

FIGURE 6.1   *Two Dimensions of Civil Association*

Among the associations I have discussed so far, official business associations like Chambers of Commerce fall at the formal end, and the everyday webs of real connections so important to both Taiwanese and Chinese business fall at the informal end. The new Taiwanese Buddhist groups fall at the far formal end in religion, with the pietistic sects close behind, and ghost worship far at the other side. Community temples themselves fall in between. They are supposed to register with the government in both China and Taiwan (although many smaller temples shirk this duty in both places), and larger temples have formal organizations. Yet most of what they do has had no official or legal sanction in the twentieth century. In fact, temple plazas serve in some towns as the functional equivalent of Habermasian coffeehouses: an arena for public discussion, but without any of the formal organizational apparatus of a developed civil society.

The other dimension speaks to modernity's alleged destruction of earlier, more communal social ties in favor of voluntary association. While these newer principles of organization are indeed important, the material I have been discussing reminds us that they have not at all displaced earlier kinds of ties, which continue to thrive. The Compassionate Relief Merit Society looks very modern in these terms; it is a voluntary association of individuals. Nongovernmental organizations (NGOs), which I will discuss in this chapter, also fit this model. Ghost worship in Taiwan is just as voluntary (although not at all formal), and its popularity is also a modern phenomenon. On the other hand, communal ties of kith and kin remain centrally important in both China and Taiwan. We see this in the importance of kinship for business connections, in the new rise of lineages in China, and in the continuing importance of local community temples. The personal connections so important across the region have their roots in both voluntary and communal ties, and it is worth recalling that the same thing was true long before the twentieth century. This is a kind of semicommunal area, where people draw on ties of neighborhood and kinship to construct networks.

Placing these kinds of ties on a chart like Figure 6.1 means greatly simplifying everything, but it also clarifies some patterns. First, it is worth noting that the upper right-hand quadrant is empty. In principle it should hold formally organized associations based on communal ties. In practice such organizations have had a very difficult time in the twentieth century. The most obvious earlier organizations of this kind were lineages, place of origin associations, and guilds. Guilds no longer exist, and the others have been largely transformed. Lineages, for example, still exist and may have formal hierarchies and rules. Yet these formalities do not have government backing and so exist only on a base of very local, informal social connections. In addition, the very large and powerful lineages that once dominated life in parts of southeast China were thoroughly undercut after the Revolution. Lineages appear to be undergoing something of a rebirth there, but more as local and officially unrecognized communal ties than as formal organizations.[2] Single surname associations (*tongxing hui*), distant cousins to lineages, are again important in cities, but they are legally structured as voluntary associations, and in fact work on a voluntary basis, not a communal one. Joining a surname association is simply an option for individuals with the right name, but these associations are not an inevitable fact of life like lineages. Much the same is true now for place of origin associations (*tongxiang hui*), which are just one of many options for people in cities now. China's village committees (*cunmin weiyuanhui*) and urban street committees (*jiedao weiyuanhui*) have a formal existence, but only as direct creations of the government. They are not based on communal ties independent of the state.

Formal communal institutions are absent from Figure 6.1 because they are the dual victims of modernity. To an extent, they suffer from the atomized social relations and increased individualism of all modern societies. While I have argued that such processes are far less thorough than has sometimes been claimed, they are nevertheless real. Perhaps even more importantly, modernist states—of both the socialist and capitalist varieties—have not made room for such organizations in their legal and administrative frameworks. They continue to exist, but have been pushed increasingly into the informal social sector.[3]

A second observation that comes from identifying these two dimensions of associational life is that much of the literature on modernity and civil society limits itself to the upper left-hand quadrant of Figure 6.1.

This bias toward the formal and voluntary end has a theoretical justification in the ties of the concept "civil society" to Enlightenment notions of the individual. Under the modernist assumption that communal ties must lose their power, academic and political attention has focused on the voluntary side. This also reflects a methodological convenience—these kinds of groups are easiest to track through quantitative surveys or government registration records. As an example, Putnam's influential "Bowling Alone" article relies almost exclusively on survey information about voting patterns and formal, voluntary associations (Boy Scouts, PTA, fraternal associations, and so on).[4] Informal ties are largely ignored. Even the bowling example makes the problem clear. He has empirical evidence that there are fewer formally organized bowling leagues in the United States, but bowling lanes get as much use as ever, and this is almost always by people in groups, in spite of the title of his article. The alternative to bowling in formal teams is bowling in informal groups, not bowling alone. An equivalent prejudice characterizes studies of "civil society" in Eastern Europe and China, which tend to concentrate on NGOs and other formal, voluntary groups, while ignoring the reservoirs of informal social capital that I have argued are so important in China and Taiwan.[5]

Formal and informal associations serve some of the same functions, but their potential for social influence is not the same. Formal associations can best organize themselves to lobby government offices because they have clear structures that the state recognizes. Yet they can also most easily be co-opted or simply repressed for exactly the same reasons. This is in fact the pattern that has characterized most Chinese societies in the twentieth century, where a roughly corporatist model characterized Singapore; Taiwan, until martial law was lifted in 1987; Hong Kong, until the tardy reforms of the last few years before the handover; and increasingly the People's Republic of China. From the material I have been discussing, this effect appears clearly in the political and social conservatism of the formal and voluntary religious associations like Compassionate Relief or the Way of Unity. It is just as clear in the reluctance of big business associations, with their strong ties to officials, to push for fundamental political change in Taiwan or Hong Kong.

In practice this often leaves only the informal sector to serve as an independent source of social capital. By its nature, this sector is less well organized to promote national change, but, as Taiwan shows, it is also the resource out of which a formal civil sector can be created when the state steps back. The communal and semicommunal end of the informal sector is especially important in this because the voluntary end really does tend to dissolve into individualism if there is no formal structure—ghost worship is not likely to develop into a broader social movement, but kinship ties or local temples certainly can, as I will show in a moment. This relatively informal and communal end of things defends social capital against the threats of modernity and authoritarian rule. It maintains a social world against the push to atomize the world, and against total incorporation by an increasingly powerful state. The social world, sometimes pushed into the narrow interstices between market and state, can nevertheless take the lead in promoting change.

Taiwan's Environmental Movement

Taiwan's powerful environmental movement shows how this can evolve. Twenty years ago the Taiwanese rarely voiced concern about environmental problems, and seemed heedless of issues that were already rocking the West and Japan.[6] Yet now "garbage wars" over the placement of sanitary landfills threaten the island with mounds of uncollected refuse, large and well-organized protest movements have seriously delayed nuclear power plant and oil refinery construction, and a wide range of environmental organizations—from the Taiwan branch of Greenpeace to the Environmental Mamas—organizes people toward new attitudes and policies. The government itself, long considered oblivious to environmental issues, now produces educational cartoons on environmental protection.

Environmental protest mushroomed in the late 1980s, and just the three years between 1988 and 1990 saw over NT$12 billion (about US$500 million) paid to settle environmental lawsuits.[7] The economic impact, of course, goes far beyond direct reparations, as the island begins to deal with the legacy of decades of rapid growth with little concern for the consequences, and as more polluting industries consider moving their investment elsewhere. The environment has grown into a major issue in many local elections. It also causes an occasional scandal, as when the president was found to patronize several illegal and environmentally unsound golf courses.[8]

This sudden surge in the environment as an issue—in fact a metamorphosis in how nature itself is conceived—responds in part to the simple facts of pollution. Protesters complain of foul gas emissions that force their children from school, stunted crops from the polluted air and ground, and tap water that ignites at the touch of a match. "Sanitary landfills," the most volatile issue recently, are usually neither sanitary nor landfills, but just great heaps of garbage.

At the same time, this new awareness of the environment grows from the tensions and changes of modernity itself. Western environmentalism has its most immediate roots in nineteenth-century reactions to modernity, from Thoreau's partial withdrawal from the world of social commerce to Muir's half-religious communion with the wilderness.[9] As in the West, the move to the cities, the mechanization of daily life, the commodification of human relationships, and a general feeling of alienation from both nature and tradition contribute to the new appreciation of nature in Taiwan. Thus, in addition to the environmental movement, Taiwan has had a recent surge in nature tourism, nature publishing, and earlier ways of relating to nature like geomancy.

National Environmental Groups

As in many countries, Taiwan's environmental movement has two faces. The first is local and ad hoc, reacting to an immediate need and then usually dissolving. The second consists of island-wide groups with a standing commitment to environmental issues. Members of these groups tend to be urban, highly educated, and quite secular. They easily fit into a stereotype of Western civil organizations, with clearly formalized structures built on a voluntary membership of individuals. International organizations like Greenpeace and Earthday have had a direct influence. Both policymakers and environmental leaders tend to have Western graduate degrees, and both speak most clearly in familiar Western idioms of economic growth versus environmental protection.

Most of the current major environmental organizations—the New Environment Foundation, Taiwan Greenpeace, the Taiwan Environmental Protection Union (TEPU), and the Homemakers' Union Environmental Protection Foundation—were founded within months after martial law was lifted in 1987.[10] All of these organizations shared comparable goals. As TEPU put it in their newsletter, they were "based on the principle of uniting people who care about protecting the environment in all regions and fields of work, jointly promoting the environmental protection movement and preserving Taiwan's ecology."[11]

Academics dominate the island-wide leadership of environmentalism in Taiwan. Both New Environment and Taiwan Greenpeace, for example, have developed into organizations run by and for small groups of perhaps a hundred academics. Neither has a significant grassroots membership, and both primarily sponsor academic lectures and similar events. When they join protest movements, it is mainly to lend their academic weight and public influence (which is sometimes considerable) to the largest issues, like opposition to nuclear power. They do not actually go out and· organize. Most environmental activists described them to me as relatively moribund, run by important public figures who helped found the movement, but who have now moved on to other forums. Edgar Lin (Lin Junyi), the founder of Taiwan Greenpeace, for example, chose to pursue electoral office as a way of promoting his goals, which has left the organization with little attention.[12] He has still more recently helped found the Green Consumer's Foundation.

TEPU, in contrast, remains extremely active in a wide range of protest movements, and sees itself ideally as an umbrella for local grassroots organizations. They have branches all over the island, led by local activists rather than national academics. Often these local branches focus on a small but stable leadership that has crystallized out of a major demonstration.[13] Their total membership in 1992 was about 1,200. Yet it would be a mistake to think of them as an organic outgrowth of local movements. Academics dominate TEPU's leadership. The chair has always been an academic, and their academic advisory committee is guaranteed 30 percent of the seats on their executive committee. It was founded by a group of eminent academics, not as a union of local leaders.

Liu Zhicheng, the chair in 1992, is a good example. He is a chemical engineer with an American Ph.D., specializing in toxicology. He describes his commitment to the environment as growing in Taiwan, first from an undergraduate course he had, and then from developments in Taiwan after he returned from the United States in the late 1980s. Yet whatever their origins, his attitudes clearly resonate easily with Western environmentalism. He sees a conflict between economic growth and environmental protection, and feels that the economy should be secondary. He argues that new growth should be halted at least temporarily while the damage is repaired, and allowed again only if ways are found to grow without doing new harm. His priorities thus lie in a kind of equilibrated nature, seen in opposition to human expansion. This is quite different from the progrowth views that Taiwanese often express in opinion polls.

Nearly all the major players in these new debates have been men. Yet there are also important women's environmental groups, which often have a much larger social base. Unlike the men, the women's groups often root their actions in dissatisfaction with family life. As extended families become less viable, especially in crowded cities, women's own career needs often directly interfere with what they see as their family responsibilities and even with their marriage possibilities. At the same time, nonworking wives in wealthy families share a new desire for fulfillment beyond the family. The answer has been a reassertion of women's traditional responsibility for nurturing children and fostering a uterine family, but taken beyond the family to the society at large, as I discussed in the preceding chapter. The environment offers a platform for these interests as easily as Compassionate Merit's philanthropy. Women involved in organized environmental groups have also tended toward philanthropic women's and religious associations. These groups are more interested in improving society than in generating new moral philosophies, again like Compassionate Relief, and that in itself recalls traditional gender differences.

The most important such group in Taiwan has been the Homemakers' Union Environmental Protection Foundation. Many of their original leaders were the wives of leading academic and political environmentalists, and most of the group are middle-class (or higher) women in their thirties and forties, generally with a college education.[14] Organizational policy is to serve women who are married but not employed. In spite of their intimate ties to the academic environmental groups, the Homemakers' Union pursues an independent path. With a popular base in middle-class housewives, they are not willing to take on controversial political issues, and are not interested in the more strictly academic lectures and roundtables of the other groups. Unlike the other national environmental groups, which are mostly male and mostly American Ph.D.s, they try to root their environmentalism in issues of household and motherhood. As Lu Hwei-syin has discussed, the stock Chinese image of the nurturing mother plays a pivotal role in their imagery. Their introductory brochure thus shows an image of a woman pushing the bandaged earth in a wheelchair, with the slogan, "Women take care of the wounded earth."[15]

Most predominantly for them, environmental protection is a means to defend the health of their children. Following this logic, the Homemakers' Union uses the term "environment" in an extremely broad sense. For example, they run summer camps for children, organize very popular meetings on child-rearing practices, and publish books encouraging children to be more independent, especially as a way of discouraging molestation and abuse. All of this falls under the heading of "spiritual environment" *(xinling huanjing)*.

Taipei's Jinghua Social and Cultural Education Foundation is a religious example of the same sort of association. They were founded by a Chan monk late in 1990, mostly to promote social education, combat pornography, and help troubled youth. They include an Environmental Protection Committee, which functions with relative independence. The head of the committee, Wu Muxin, experimented with Christianity and other religions in college, and took lay Buddhist vows some years later.[16] Her experience with environmental organizations began with the largely academic New Environment, and their board of directors still overlaps with New Environment to an extent. As she said, however, she felt out of place among all those intellectuals. She also felt that their research orientation distracted them from real work at the grassroots. She went from New Environment to the Homemakers' Union, but had problems there because she works, and most of their activities take place during the day.

She joined Jinghua in 1991, and helped form the Environmental Protection Committee. They began with roundtables and discussion meetings, but have been moving toward other mechanisms that might meet broader audiences. They are beginning to do more public lectures, and have been organizing flea markets, allowing people to sell or exchange their old things instead of throwing them away. She also has a personal interest in promoting green products like battery rechargers or reusable shopping bags. They aim primarily at family issues and at religious audiences.

The similarity to the Homemakers' Union issues comes as no surprise given Wu's background, but the Buddhism provides two important differences. First, the structure of Buddhism provides an alternative form of organization. Wu tries to recruit important Buddhist masters to promote the cause. A famous master might have hundreds of disciples, and could easily attract hundreds to a lecture. Some have television audiences in addition. Many of these followers are older people who might otherwise be difficult for environmentalists to reach. No other kind of environmental organization has access to the same kind of social network. Second, Jinghua justifies its stand on environmental protection from within Buddhism, rather than through Chinese family values.[17] Buddhism, after all, forbids killing any living thing. The Buddha-nature exists everywhere and in everything, which is used here to justify a kind of ecological equilibrium. Compassionate Relief's emphasis on simplicity has also led it to address environmental issues, mostly recycling, as a secondary goal.[18]

Local Movements—Informal and Communal Ties

National environmental organizations take different forms depending on whether men or women dominate. All of them, however, are formal, voluntary associations of the kind usually associated with civil society. Yet as soon as we look beyond those top ranks, the environmental movement takes on specifically Taiwanese cultural forms and social organization with deep local roots. In particular, kinship and community religion can play crucial organizational roles.

It can be difficult to mobilize local temples to support environmental protest, given their intimate symbolic and organizational ties to local authority. Yet when temples can be won over, they offer the movement a powerful moral sanction in local terms, alongside a ready-made organizational network and a stockpile of funds. Both sides may try to mobilize religion. When Formosa Plastics decided to build Taiwan's sixth naphtha cracker (a large and often polluting industrial plant that refines oil products into precursors of plastics) in Yunlin, Y. C. Wang (Wang Yongqing)—CEO and one of the wealthiest men in Taiwan—called on each of the major local temples and offered a generous donation. Apparently as a result, none of them have become involved in local protests.[19]

Protests against Taiwan's fifth naphtha cracker, however, made very effective use of religion. This plant was to be built in the Houjing neighborhood of Gaoxiong City by China Petrochemicals, in a large refining complex already there.[20] Protesters had blockaded the west-side gate to the compound soon after the new plant was proposed in 1987. The blockade continued through the next two years, supplemented by occasional blockades of the main gate after alarming incidents—once after one of the leaders was beaten and robbed by a drunk China Petrochemicals employee, and again after extraordinary emissions from the main refinery.

Cai Chaopeng, one of the main leaders of the movement, had run a fortune-telling business before the protests, and had wide experience with spirit writing and other forms of Taiwanese religion. Liu Yongling, another top leader, told me that they had asked one of their major local gods—Shen Nong, the god of agriculture—for support at the very beginning. They used the simplest method of divination, throwing two curved pieces of bamboo root (Hokkien *poe*), which can come up "yes," "no," or "laughing." Defying the odds, he says it came up "yes" nine times in a row. When the KMT tried it, he says, the result was always "no." Probably more critically, Cai managed to garner financial backing from this temple in August 1987—it gave NT$2 million (nearly US$100,000) to the protest committee.

The most creative use of local temple religion came in December of that year. As Cai Chaopeng and Liu Yongling told it, the protesters had left a handful of people to keep watch over the banner that represented their blockade of China Petrochemicals. Plainclothes police came by late at night, bringing alcoholic gifts. When the sentries finally passed out, the police removed the banner, symbolically ending the blockade. A thousand riot police were out in force the next day to prevent a renewal of the blockade. When the protest committee discovered this in the morning, they used the temple public address system to call people together. Religion provided an ideal mechanism to reestablish the blockade, because religious parades, unlike other forms of public demonstration, usually receive rubber-stamp official permission.

As part of their show of religious force, the group mobilized the temple's traditional martial arts performing group, a Songjiang Zhen, to support them while they set up a spirit altar at the gate. These performing groups involve dozens of young martial arts enthusiasts, armed with spears and swords, who perform traditional routines at important festivals. They wear operatic costumes and makeup, and their steps are ritualized. Nevertheless, the weapons are real, the performers can fight, and the element of real physical threat was obvious to everyone.[21] The police had to back down, and in the end the protesters agreed to take the spirit altar down in return for the right to leave their banner (and the blockade) up.

The other crucial religious intercession occurred on May 5, 1990. This was the eve of a local referendum on building the plant. Everyone expected a victory for China Petrochemicals; 81 percent of people polled nationally supported building the plant. The forces most adamantly opposed to construction gathered less than one hundred people to worship the god of agriculture and ask his preference in the referendum. Again they threw *poe*, and again they got a powerful response of eleven straight agreements with the most radical position against construction. As word of this minor miracle got out, a crowd began to build, finally developing to perhaps a thousand people. Most of them made incense offerings to the temple, and the contents of the incense pot eventually burst into a large fire. This phenomenon is called *hoat lo* (manifesting the incense pot, Mandarin *fa lu*), and people consider it a powerful acknowledgment of the deity's approval.

Further enhancing the power of the event, the goddess Guanyin suddenly possessed an older woman. Putting her fingers into the lotus mudra, the goddess/woman began chanting that the Houjing neighborhood would be doomed if the plant were built. Such spirit possession is not at all unusual in Taiwan, and provides a powerful possibility for mobilizing religious authority, since the normally conservative authorities who manage temples cannot control what their god says through a medium. After the fact, many people credited this single event with the results of the next day—people voted to oppose the naphtha cracker without compromise. In the end, the government ignored the referendum and approved construction, but the long protest did succeed in pushing the company to set up a NT$1.5 billion (about US$60 million) foundation to benefit Houjing, and to promise extensive investment in pollution control. The blockade of the west side gate was lifted in November 1990, after 1,202 days.[22]

As protectors of community welfare, and often as symbols of community opposed to national or other interests, local deities provide easy cultural opportunities for social movements. Religion, in addition, offers an established social network that can be mobilized. Indeed, temples and political factions together (and sometimes kinship) provide the main lines through which leaders can normally mobilize local people. They are not classic civil society organizations, but they provide exactly the kinds of informal ties that can become important in the construction of a new civil society under conditions like Taiwan's lifting of martial law in 1987.

Winning the support of the local temple thus added a powerful social network and symbol of community well-being to this movement. Others have been less spectacular, but just as effective. One Gaoxiong county community successfully opposed a garbage dump when the temple realized that its main deity, a plague god (Ong Ia), would have to set sail in an important annual ritual in polluted water. In another case, the local temple in Dalinpu, Gaoxiong City, finally supported the long and angry protests against Taiwan Power, China Petrochemicals, and China Steel, but only after a riot. The temple agreed to pay bail (over NT$100,000) for people arrested, primarily because the accused rioters included a relative of one of the temple management-committee members.[23]

Local environmental movements in Taiwan also often pick up the language and social networks of kinship and make use of symbolism from family ritual, especially funerals. Demands to save resources for descendants resonate deeply with Chinese ideals of filial piety, and mesh with economic behavior that attempts to maximize an estate to be handed down to future generations. The frequent borrowing of funeral symbolism in protests furthers this image of filial piety, and rebuts state or corporate worries about economic growth with the classical Chinese value of filial piety. This is another case of drawing on earlier kinds of values as a response to perceived exploitation through the market. At the same time, however, "family" has never been the same to all Taiwanese, and gender differences in kinship experience show up in how men and women talk about the environment, just as they do in economic discourse about Confucian values.

The central idea of a duty to provide for descendants as the only way of continuing the lineage can conveniently shape environmental rhetoric, even though it (like religion) is inherently particularistic and local in appeal. A fishermen's protest in Hualian, for example, put out a brochure called "Protect Hualian's Shore for our Children and Grandchildren." It read, in part: "Dear people of Hualian County, teachers, mothers: Let us unite for the sake of our beloved sons and daughters, and absolutely oppose the China Paper factory, which continues to poison Hualian's seas and air."

Most uses of these terms are more gender laden than this brochure. One example strikes anyone passing through the site of the proposed fourth nuclear power generator, planned for the northeast coast of Taipei County. Opponents have lined the road leading through the area with signs. Probably half of them denounce the plant as a threat to the local people's descendants. When I interviewed Jiang Qunhe, one of the local leaders, he also frequently talked about the importance of preserving the area as a patrimony for his descendants. The term for descendants here is *zisun*, literally children and grandchildren, or sons and grandsons. Such sentiments appear over and over in grassroots environmental organizing.[24] *Zisun* was also the word used in the title of the brochure from Hualian. Frequent use of such language at local levels clearly reverberates with men's lineage ideals and a general dedication to filial piety.

Typically, the main organizers against the nuclear power plant are men, and the author of the Hualian brochure was also male.

Funeral ritual is the most public enactment of filial piety, and funeral symbolism often shows up in Taiwanese protests. Funerals have a broad back for carrying protest in many parts of the world, but seem especially prone to re-readings as protest in East Asia. They run a wide range from the conversion of official mourning to political protest in the People's Republic of China, to the South Korean borrowing of funerals of slain student demonstrators as forums for pushing democratic reforms, to the use of standard funeral symbols like white headbands and banners, pioneered in Japan but now spread throughout East Asian protest movements.[25]

Taiwan echoes these same themes, as the idea of filial piety helps to justify protest in widely held and politically acceptable values. As the most obvious visible commemoration of the debt owed to ancestors and the obligation owed to children, funeral ritual is a natural carrier for environmental protest. In most cases, the funerals treat the local land, river, or sea as a dead parent, trying to claim the moral high ground in these battles. By implication, holding such a funeral accuses the state or company of murdering the environment. At the same time, the "mourners" claim an expanded filial piety in response to the usual accusations that protesters are just out for financial compensation.

Sometimes protest funerals borrow another occasion for mourning, instead of mourning the land directly. One of the most influential occurred during Houjing's march to reopen their blockade, which I just discussed. The martial arts display accompanied a funeral. They carried four coffins, intending to set up a spirit altar back at the west gate of the factory compound, and thus reestablish their blockade. This "funeral" was nominally to commemorate the death of a man who had recently immolated himself in Taibei over other issues entirely. Typically, these coffins suggested the idea of mourning for a slain environment, just as they conjured up images of the discarded Confucian responsibility to the welfare of future generations. They also added an element of threat, because the group carried the traditional funeral wreaths, but wrote the names of factory managers on them, instead of the name of the dead man.

These death rituals further the idea that the environment is part of an estate which must be passed along to descendants. Women in Taiwan, however, tend to take a different view of what kinship is about, as I have discussed. In local movements as in national organizations, women tend to stress nurturing nature much more than creating a patrimony for sons and grandsons. One of the scholars at the Academia Sinica, for example, made a speech protesting the proposed construction of a sanitary landfill nearby. Towing her children along to make her point, she even borrowed a couple of extras to help the image along. She clearly felt that her authority as mother and caretaker would carry more weight than her position as scholar and professional, and happily pointed out afterwards that she had been taken for a housewife. This call to more global issues of general nurturance marks the earth both as mother to us all, and as sick child in need of loving care. This strategy downplays the male appeal to patrimony, heirs, and local resources.

Thus large demonstrations, which are mostly run by men, often talk in generalities about preserving the world for their descendants. Such language promotes neither a nature for its own sake nor a general love of humanity; instead it builds on the old Chinese reverence for the patriline. Women's involvement, in contrast, tends to emphasize the household itself over the lineage. This universalizing theme fits easily with the national organizations run by women, with its emphasis on nurturance of children and of the earth itself.[26]

All these changes, for men and women both, indicate a growing local political autonomy, in which organization from below has a much greater chance to mobilize resources than ever before. Local self-help organizations, for all their ties to machine politics and occasionally even local hoodlums, appear to be signs of new kinds of local incentive not possible under the earlier authoritarian regime. They parallel in many ways early environmental organizations in Japan, which pioneered efforts in local political mobilization.[27]

Leaders of the national groups, the ones at the formal and voluntary corner of Figure 6.1, generally feel a great distance from tradition-bound local religious and kinship practice, exactly because those techniques rely on informal and at least partially communal ties. These practices do not fit well either with the Western-educated intellectuals who run those organizations, or with environmentalist universals. Typical of modernizing elites anywhere, they generally feel ambivalent at best about practices that seem premodern to them, especially in the forms most effective in actual movements: possessed mediums, flaming incense pots, powerful divinations. Just as importantly, they reject the localism and particularism inherent in the use of religion and kinship. The gods of local temples above all protect their immediate human communities, as lineages protect their members; they worry about the environment only when it threatens their people. This parochialism offers little encouragement for a global or even an island-wide view of ecology. Thus while local religion and kinship have actively helped build a civil society in Taiwan, and helped shape policy from the grassroots, they remain tied to purely local interests. The most "modern" sector is thus uncomfortable with them, even though they have also had an enormous impact on policy. Both sectors have pushed forward the lines of democratic civility in Taiwan.

Learning Curves

Examining the pattern of environmental protest over time in Taiwan further reveals the social base of civil action, and shows how sensitively social movements interact with each other and with government policy. Figure 6.2 shows the general pattern in environmental protest from 1979 through 1991. The very rapid increase after martial law was lifted in 1987 comes as no surprise, but the graph also shows a small number of protests even in the relatively repressive year of 1979, with steady increases throughout the first part of the 1980s.[28] The first successful environmental lawsuit took place in 1981, and other protests led to eight steel mills being shut down in Taipei.[29] This reflected in part a bit more free space for social action that the government was allowing then. Environmental action can also claim to be strictly apolitical, which allowed this movement (and others, like the consumer protection movement) more leeway from the state than anything that claimed a political agenda.

The patterns that follow show a clear learning curve (see Figures 6.3 and 6.4). For example, the proportion of cases with radical demands—that polluting factories be moved or shut down, or that a new location be found for the village itself—roughly halved during the 1980s (Figure 6.3). This decline in radical goals responds simply to what worked. Drastic demands for the removal of factories or whole villages made it more difficult to mobilize support—major local polluters are also usually major local employers, and most public opinion favors continued industrial growth. In addition, most such attempts ran up against an official stone wall. As people learned that more modest demands had greater chances of success, they changed their strategies. Requests for compensation or reform tended to be much more successful.

While the nature of the demands has softened over time, the techniques of protest actually grew increasingly confrontational between 1979 and 1990. Extralegal techniques (street demonstrations, blockades, riots) increased to over 50 percent (see Figure 6.4). Although petitions continued to be used in about a quarter of the cases throughout the period, other officially sanctioned techniques fell from favor. Formal revelations to officials (*fanying*), formal accusations (*jianju*), and mediation hearings (*xietiao hui*) had nearly disappeared from the repertoire by 1990. The most striking increase was in blockades, where people physically blocked entrances to factories, construction sites, or garbage dumps,

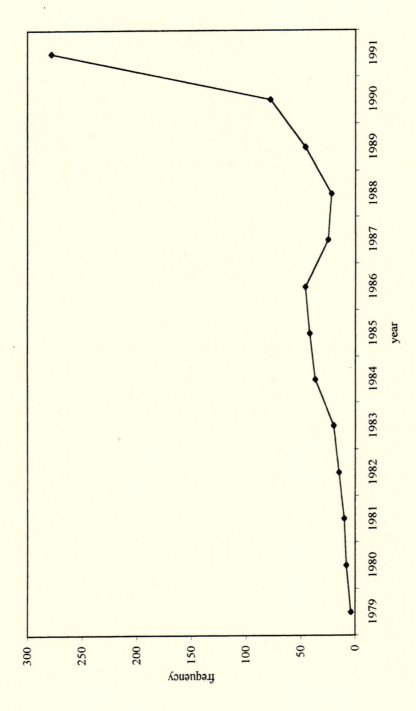

FIGURE 6.2   Frequency of Environmental Protest in Taiwan, 1979–1991

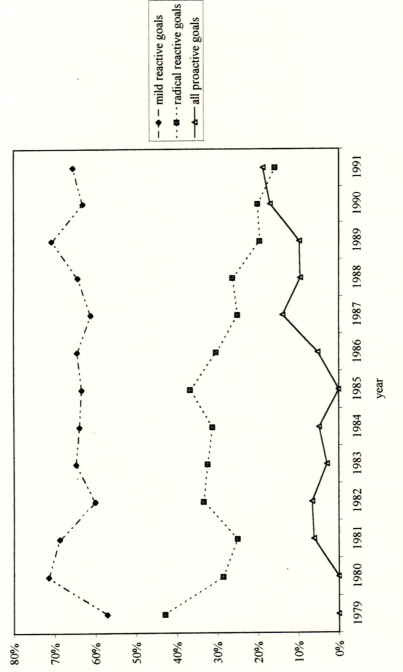

FIGURE 6.3 *Types of Protest Goals (as % of all goals)*

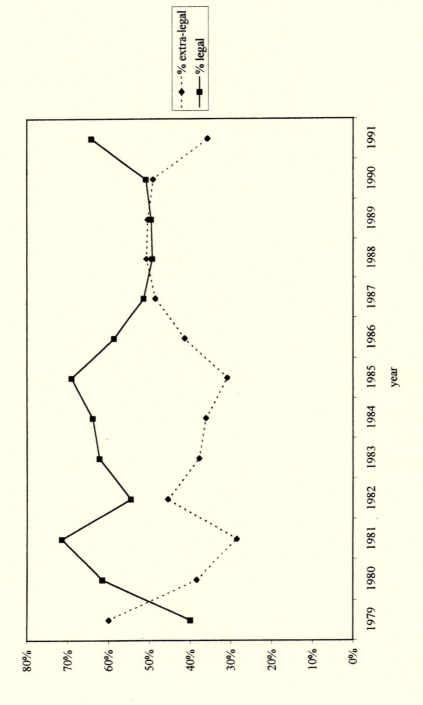

FIGURE 6.4 *Legal versus Extralegal Techniques (as % of all techniques)*

sometimes maintaining the siege for months or years (like the naphtha cracker in Houjing). Nearly a quarter of the cases used blockades by the end of the period.

The explanation for this pattern again lies in a kind of pragmatic negotiation through action, as protesters learned what might work, what was ignored, and what brought down the wrath of the law. People began with peaceful and legalistic methods, which simply had little effect on an unsympathetic government. This led to an escalation in techniques, especially after martial law was lifted. The government would not tolerate riots, which they considered chaotic threats to public order. Yet they would allow extralegal techniques like blockades that kept the battle orderly (usually) and tied to the local area. Thus while the legal and political apparatus rarely came to the aid of protesters, the government did allow private solutions beyond the limits of the law.

The pattern changed again in 1991, at the same time as the number of protests increased so heavily. Legal techniques suddenly increased again, especially the use of formal revelation and public hearings. Blockades decreased, and the entire statistical pattern looks more like the early 1980s. Yet the reasons for the pattern were quite different in 1991. The explanation lies in a change in government policy, as the Taiwan Environmental Protection Agency became more responsive to public demands in 1991. Word very quickly spread that working through official channels could be effective for the kinds of moderate demands (often for compensation) that people were now usually making. Adjustment of strategies took place very quickly.

The frequency of protests is thus not just a simple function of the opening of more civil space by a retreating authoritarian state. The changing state was of course a critical factor: only the most desperate dared a protest under Chiang Kai-shek. Yet the numbers of protests relate more closely to an interplay between state and popular pressures. They show a lively dynamic where politicians, environmentalists, and local residents play off each other's moves, constantly adjusting their strategies and goals.

These findings help put the rapid changes of 1987 in context. Although the government clearly played an important role in moving Taiwan to democracy, much of the social base already existed in the local communities that could mobilize to pursue their interests and influence policy. Formal associations like environmental NGOs had no real place under martial law, but the social capital for Taiwan's future civil society was already developing out of local community ties. The environmental and other movements began to mobilize that social capital in interaction with the state well before martial law was lifted, and they prepared the ground for Taiwan's booming civil world in the 1990s.

The People's Republic

The split between a formal, voluntary, nationally organized sector and an informal, more communal sector is even starker in China than in Taiwan. China's socialist legacy and its current move toward corporatist patterns have helped remove anything in the middle. As we have already seen for associational life in business and religion, the choices tend to be between large organizations with close ties to high officials, and small-scale sets of informal ties beyond the gaze of the state.

Large-Scale Organizations

China's older national associations have their roots in socialist mass organizations like the union or the Women's Federation. These meshed directly with the government and Party at all levels, and originally had no real independence. With the recent market reforms, some of these groups have been thrown more on their own fiscal devices, and this has led in some cases to more freedom of action. This has been most striking at the lowest level—the street committees whose need to support themselves has led to their becoming independent economic actors.[30] Still, organizations like these are less NGOs than GONGOs—government-organized nongovernmental organizations—a newly coined oxymoron of great use in China. One study in Guangzhou found very few "NGOs" without direct ties to officials: only 19 percent of 152 had no officials on their board of directors, and only 26 percent said they undertook no activities on behalf of government or Party units. The more independent ones were almost entirely recreational or religious.[31]

Some new groups at least look more like standard NGOs. Only a few of these address environmental issues, but they are typical of new NGOs in China. The oldest and best-known group is Friends of Nature. They were founded in 1993 by Liang Congjie. Typically, they began under the safest possible auspices, in this case as a branch of the Academy of Chinese Culture (which is part of the Chinese Academy of Social Sciences).[32] After being turned down for registration under the National Environmental Protection Agency, they convinced the Academy of Chinese Culture to sponsor them by claiming an interest in indigenous ideas of nature. In fact, however, Friends of Nature has shown very little interest in earlier Chinese views of nature, and they largely promote a conservation ethic that could be heard anywhere in the world. Liang recognizes that there are great limits on what he can accomplish if the organization is not to be banned, and has thus defined his mission largely as education. They run a children's camp in the woods, and have been active in lobbying to prevent harm to endangered species. Their membership has grown from an original 60 to about 600; like TEPU, it is mostly intellectuals.

Other registered organizations face the same pressures, and also stay with relatively safe issues. Some groups have been organized directly by government officials associated with the environment, and are registered directly under the National Environmental Protection Agency. Most prominent of these is the Professional Association for China's Environment (PACE), whose mission is also primarily informational and whose target audience is primarily academic and professional.

Two major groups were founded by women.[33] In ways reminiscent of Taiwan's Homemakers' Union or the Buddhist Jinghua Foundation, they are less tied to top academics and high officials, and more dedicated to work at the grassroots. Global Village Beijing, founded by Sheri Liao in 1996, promotes recycling and direct education through the media. Liao has run a weekly television show and also runs programs for journalists. Official limits have so far prevented her from registering as an NGO, so the organization is registered as a nonprofit company, and must pay taxes. The second group, Green Earth Volunteers (founded in 1994), has the largest public base, organizing mostly Beijing-based volunteers to undertake specific environmental projects like creating desert windbreaks. The founder, Wang Yongchen, split away from Friends of Nature due to her desire to increase the public base, especially among students. She has also been unable to register as an NGO so far. Both these groups are less intellectual-based and less officially connected than Friends of Nature or PACE. Both urge a simpler, less materialistic lifestyle, local volunteerism, and recycling. This suggests that very similar gender dynamics are taking place on both sides of the Taiwan Strait.

Nothing as oppositional as Taiwan's TEPU is possible now, although as a Chinese policy priority in the last few years, the environment provides a forum where people can begin to push the boundaries of political possibility. Other NGOs address similarly safe issues like welfare and consumer protection. All of them must stay very tame to get and retain their official registration as NGOs. It is worth noting that these were exactly the issues around which society could mobilize in Taiwan before martial law was lifted, and that even these deeply compromised NGOs are more than Taiwan had thirty years ago. Anything more directly political or confrontational must remain local and disorganized. Those who cross the line and go beyond the space defined by current policy quickly lose their platforms. The best example for environmental issues in China is Dai Qing, whose outspoken opposition to the Three Gorges dam project has made it difficult for her voice to be heard in China, and difficult to create any organization around her.

A typical example of the importance of informal government links was the campaign by Friends of Nature to save snub-nosed monkey habitat in Yunnan from logging.[34] To attract media attention, they sent a group of about 200 students, journalists, and scientists to the region to assess possible solutions. More effectively, however, Liang used his personal connections to high officials by sending letters to Vice-Premier Jiang Chunyun and Minister of Science and Technology Song Jian. This resulted in an official (but apparently unenforced) ban on logging in the area.

Environmental and other social groups either work closely with the government or are repressed. The only alternative is to remain small, disorganized, and informal. In principle China's NGOs are organized in a corporatist fashion, with one group alone to represent each administrative area. This rule is not strictly enforced, but it has added to the enormous difficulty of getting an NGO registered. The successful ones tend to have high state officials on their boards, and are often the offspring of political units—"nongovernmental" in name only.[35] Others, even when they are politically unproblematic, tend not to survive. A recent account, for example, documents the rise and demise of a historic building preservation group in Beijing (which competed with a government-run "NGO"), a Zhejiang migrant association in Beijing (which had conflicts with city officials), and a shelter for abused wives in Shanghai (which was thought to reflect badly on the local Women's Federation).[36]

Other groups are directly incorporated instead of being repressed. An early example was the Research Group on Problems of China's Agricultural Development in the early 1980s. They were mostly young urban elites who had spent time in the countryside during the Cultural Revolution. They wanted to help rural people, who had no socialist mass organization to speak for them, and they were early supporters of the responsibility system reforms in agriculture. As something like an interest group, they were attacked in 1981, but were ultimately incorporated directly into the Party-State Council rural research agencies.[37] A similar tension occurred with Wang Juntao and Chen Ziming, whose group clearly hoped to work cooperatively with the state in the late 1980s. In their case, however, the Tiananmen demonstrations of 1989 led them into opposition and ultimately prison.[38] As with Taiwan, however, even corporatist and authoritarian controlled civil association can be significant—it is much more social space than had been possible since before the Revolution, and these associations can become the seeds of future change.

Staying Local

National, formally organized associations must stay close beneath the government's wing, but that also makes them relatively easy to study.

Villages and urban neighborhoods in China also have many kinds of social movements; unlike the national associations, these often become confrontational, and often push at the outer limits of policy. They rarely receive press coverage in China, and are powerfully repressed if they try to organize on a larger or more formal scale. For these reasons, they are far harder to study.

Nevertheless, we know of many kinds of local outbursts through scattered newspaper reports and observers' accounts. These events include environmental issues, especially where severe local pollution is causing a crisis. More often, however, they involve land and taxation issues in the countryside, and problems of laid-off and retired workers in the cities. In many cases these demonstrations follow a pattern strongly reminiscent of Taiwan in its late authoritarian period. People usually begin with the limited official mechanisms available. These consist primarily of writing letters or otherwise notifying government officials that they should be investigating a problem. In recent years Chinese environmental authorities have received many thousands of letters like these, and some do generate a response.[39]

These mechanisms are primarily individual, not social. The social equivalent would be a petition, but petitions usually only appear after individual methods have failed. Authoritarian rule makes it very difficult for any organized social group to act initially. When asked why they do not act more on problems they perceive, many villagers in China refer to their lack of organization and the high costs of resistance.[40]

Letter-writing and similar attempts rarely succeed. Many complaints are dropped at that point, but sometimes they escalate to extralegal means like blockades or street demonstrations. A study of official records on 278 environmental disputes found that 47 involved forceful popular protest in rural areas.[41] This pattern again reproduces the typical Taiwan experience in the 1980s. When things escalate there is usually a move from individuals to social-based protest—isolated individuals can easily be ignored or repressed. Here we can see how the social capital stored in the informal ties of daily life can be mobilized in ways that ultimately affect policy. For example, protesters blocked the entrance to a garbage dump in 1997, saying that the odor made them sick and that a pregnant woman had been hospitalized. An earlier petition to local environmental authorities got no response.[42] In another kind of case the same year protesters clashed with police in Sichuan over low salaries and nonpayment of claims by their health insurance. They had again approached local authorities first, but received no response.[43]

The main groups in these protests tend to be residential—rural villages and urban neighborhoods. Given China's work unit structure, these areas are also united economically, either by a history of farming together

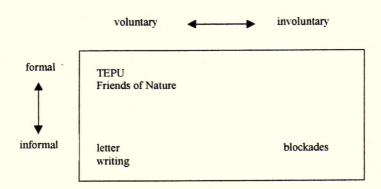

FIGURE 6.5   Examples of Environmental Action

or by working for the same unit. The mobilization of ties in units like this is one of the ironic legacies of communism, where a method of state economic and social control created a set of semicommunal ties it could not control. These networks of people who live and work together have been most obvious in the recent spate of protests after the insolvency of state-owned enterprises that are not paying full salaries or benefits, or whose failure to pay into unemployment and retirement funds for the last few years has left workers with an inadequate income. An earlier torrent of over 6,000 rural protests in 1992 and 1993 against taxation irregularities rested on village and lineage social structure. In a survey at the time, 43 percent of villagers said they could not do without the protection supplied by local lineage groups.[44]

The best understood example of this so far is the rural push for the agricultural responsibility system in the late 1970s. This took the form of organized undermining and twisting of official agricultural policy, rather than direct protest. Although elite willingness to adapt was certainly also part of the story here, the responsibility system is one case where peasant social organization clearly helped change policy.[45]

All these types of social action fit into the formal/informal and voluntary/communal distinctions I have been discussing. Figure 6.5 helps emphasize some fundamental similarities between the patterns in Taiwan and the People's Republic. As states with modernist ideologies, neither has left room for formal, communal organizations. When villages or urban districts act together, they rely on the informal social networks of kinship, religion, and neighborhood. As authoritarian regimes, both have also inadvertently fostered a wide gap between national-level formal associations and localized, ad hoc movements built on informal, communal ties. The national organizations by necessity have been politically careful, and limited to areas that do not openly challenge official policy. Local movements are far bolder. Authoritarian rule, even at extremes like the Cultural Revolution, has never been able to destroy the independent ties on which these movements are based, but they do successfully keep such movements ephemeral and local. This changed in Taiwan only after martial law was lifted in 1987, and space suddenly opened up for organizations like TEPU, and for long-term social action that mobilizes help on a large scale, like the opposition to the naphtha cracker I have discussed, or ongoing opposition to new nuclear power plant construction

Both China and Taiwan also mobilize communal or semicommunal ties of religion, family, and neighborhood at the local level. Some of these similarities, like the role of lineages and local temples, occur because of the shared cultural history of both places. There are also differences, of course, where their very separate political and economic legacies have reshaped those ties. This is clear, for example, in the importance of work-unit mobilization in China much more than in Taiwan. And in part both places are similar because, as I have been suggesting all along, these kinds of ties were always crucial to social life. An ideology of modernity may dismiss them as merely traditional, but in fact they are a fundamental part of modern society. They have actively contributed to Taiwan's major political transformation, and they have pushed policy changes in China.

Finally, a comparison of the two cases reminds us that while such organizations may provide a constant pressure on the state, they are no guarantee of democratic transformation. China is only just now allowing the kind of corporatist NGO sector that Taiwan had for decades. That is an enormous change, and will make a political transition much easier. But as Taiwan showed, a regime can continue for many years by keeping the national level tame and the local level disorganized. Such collections of social capital made Taiwan's transition to true civil society much easier, perhaps even made it possible at all, but they were hardly its sole cause.

Notes

1. I borrow the phone book metaphor from Peter Berger.

2. See Xu Wang, "Mutual Empowerment of State and Peasantry: Grassroots Democracy in Rural China," *World Development*, 25(9) (1997), pp. 1431–1442.

3. For religious policy in the early twentieth century, see Prasenjit Duara, "Knowledge and Power in the Discourse of Modernity: The Campaigns Against Popular Religion in Early Twentieth-century China," *Journal of Asian Studies*, 50(1) (1991), pp. 67–83.

4. Putnam, "Bowling Alone."

5. Ignoring the informal sector can have stark policy consequences. For example, it can help determine whether a transitional economy favors very small entrepreneurs (like Poland) or looks to a large corporate structure (like Russia).

6. Much of the research in this section was done jointly with Hsin-Huang Michael Hsiao of the Institute of Sociology at the Academia Sinica, Taiwan. We explore some of these issues further in Hsin-Huang Michael Hsiao, Lester W. Milbrath, and Robert P. Weller, "Antecedents of an Environmental Movement in Taiwan," *Capitalism, Nature, Socialism* 6(3) (1995), pp. 91–104, and Robert P. Weller and Hsin-Huang Michael Hsiao, "Culture, Gender and Community in Taiwan's Environmental Movement," in Arne Kalland and Gerard Persoon, eds., *Environmental Movements in Asia* (London: Curzon, 1998), pp. 83–109.

7. See Li Lixun, "Gonghai Jiufen Shihuaye Zhaohuoli Zui Gao [Harm Rate from Oil Industry Highest in Disputes over Damages]," *Lianhe Bao,* July 21, 1992, p. 1. The actual figure is probably higher. Lawyers in Taiwan have told me that most such cases are settled out of court.

8. "Bunkered," *The Economist,* October 23, 1993, p. 44.

9. Other strands of Western thought also underlie Western environmentalism, including medieval ideas about the Great Chain of Being (see Keith Thomas, *Man and the Natural World: A History of the Modern Sensibility* [New York: Pantheon, 1983]), elite desires to maintain and improve hunting preserves (see John M. MacKenzie, *The Empire of Nature: Hunting, Conservation and British Imperialism* [Manchester: Manchester University Press, 1988]), and colonial scientists witnessing rapid environmental change under European impact (see Richard Grove, "Conserving Eden: The [European] East India Companies and their Environmental Policies on St. Helena, Mauritius, and in Western India, 1660–1854," *Comparative Studies in Society and History,* 35[2] [1993], pp. 318–351).

10. Other organizations had existed earlier, but none wielded comparable influence. The most important was an environmental committee of the Consumer's Foundation, founded in 1984. See Zhang, *Shehui Yundong yu Zhengzhi Zhuanhua,* p. 53 for a list. The magazine *Life and Environment* began in the early 1980s, but never had a broad readership, and folded quickly. There were also other early precursors like the bird-watching societies in various cities and counties.

11. Shi Xinmin, "Fakan Ci [Editor's Introduction]," *Taiwan Huanjing [Taiwan Environment]* 1(1) (1988), pp. 1–3.

12. I will take up the Homemakers' Union separately below. As an organization exclusively for women, especially housewives, it differs significantly from the academic (and mostly male) enclaves I discuss in this section.

13. Thus the Gaoxiong branch grew out of the failed opposition to China Petrochemicals' Number Five Naphtha Cracker, the Northwest branch out of opposition to the Number Four Nuclear Power Plant, and the Ilan branch out of successful opposition to Formosa Plastics' proposed naphtha cracker.

14. See Lu, "Women's Self-growth Groups." Information in this section is also based on my interview with Lin Yupei, the general secretary, in 1992.

15. Ibid., p. 34.

16. This information comes from Jinghua publications and from an interview with Wu Muxin, July 13, 1992.

17. In fact, the relation of Buddhism to filial piety has always been problematic in China, where monastic celibacy combined with a willingness to make offerings to anyone's ancestors pitted Buddhists against traditionalists.

18. See Zhang, "Fuojiao Ciji Gongde Hui."

19. This is based on interviews conducted near the construction site, August 1993.

20. This summary is based on newspaper reports for the period, interviews with some local residents, and interviews with Cai Chaopeng and Liu Yongling, two of the top leaders of the protest, in July 1992.

21. Rumor also spoke of Molotov cocktails, although I cannot confirm it.

22. This example is discussed in more detail in Weller and Hsiao "Culture, Gender and Community," along with several other similar cases.

23. This is based on interviews with participants, July 1992.

24. The term *zisun* can include both genders, but the implications of a Confucian male line are clear. Reversing the two characters into *sunzi*, for instance, makes the word for grandsons, excluding granddaughters who must be specified as female (*sunnü*).

25. See Weller, *Resistance*, pp. 191–194, for a more extended discussion of this phenomenon.

26. See Lu, "Women's Self-growth Groups," pp. 34–35.

27. Margaret A. McKean, *Environmental Protest and Citizen Politics in Japan* (Berkeley: University of California Press, 1981).

28. Repression was strong in 1979 in part because the United States had broken diplomatic relations on January 1. Elections the previous fall had been cancelled, and a major opposition magazine was shut down early that year. Its leaders were given long jail terms of hard labor. There was some loosening during the early 1980s, but the general authoritarian pattern remained until 1987.

29. See Juju Chin-Shou Wang, "Economic Growth with Pollution: Taiwan's Environmental Experience," in Uday Desai, ed., *Ecological Policy and Politics in Developing Countries: Economic Growth, Democracy, and Environment* (Albany, N.Y.: State University of New York Press, 1998), p. 130.

30. See Li, "Changing Kinship."

31. Kin-man Chan and Qiu Haixiong, "Small Government, Big Society: Social Organizations and Civil Society in China," *China Area Studies Series* (Japan) 8 (1998), pp. 34–47.

32. Information on Friends of Nature is based on his public presentations, and on a brief interview when he was in the United States.

33. For a more detailed and very useful discussion of these groups, see Evan Osnos, "An Analysis of China's Environmental NGOs: Group Involvement in the Emergence of Civil Society" (senior honors thesis, Harvard University, 1999).

34. See ibid., p. 39.

35. Qu Geping is the most important such sponsor for environmental organizations. He has a long history of promoting environmental issues within the government, and currently heads an environmental law working group of the National People's Congress. He is on the board of Friends of Nature and several other associations, and money from an international prize he won supported the founding of PACE. PACE is the offspring of the National Environmental Protection Agency. The most successful NGO is probably Project Hope, which does charity work in poor areas, and is the creation of the Youth Federation.

36. See Matt Forney, "Voice of the People," *Far Eastern Economic Review* (May 7, 1998), pp. 10–12.

37. This case is documented in Thomas P. Bernstein, "Incorporating Group Interests into the Policy Process: The Case of Farmers During the Reform Era" (paper presented to the conference on "The Non-Economic Impact of China's Economic Reforms", Harvard University, 1996), pp. 16–17.

38. Edward X. Gu, "'Non-Establishment' Intellectuals, Public Space, and the Creation of Non-Governmental Organizations in China: The Chen Ziming-Wang Juntao Saga," *China Journal* 39 (1998), pp. 39–58.

39. See Susmita Dasgupta and David Wheeler, "Citizen Complaints as Environmental Indicators: Evidence from China," Report to PRDEI, World Bank, 1996.

40. This is one of the preliminary findings of a large study of environmental policy in Anhui in which I am involved. Lianjiang Li and Kevin J. O'Brien, "Villagers and Popular Resistance in Contemporary China," *Modern China* 22(1) (1996), pp. 28–61, make a similar observation. The authors also identify a class of "recalcitrants" who sometimes escalate on their own by refusing to pay taxes or otherwise vocally not complying. In these cases, the government can usually simply repress them and be done with the problem. Such radical individual action also rarely attracts much broader social support. These are social isolates who are rarely successful.

41. Jun Jing, "Environmental Protests in Rural China," in Mark Selden and Elizabeth Perry, eds., *Social Protests in China* (New York: Routledge, forthcoming). Similar to my findings in Taiwan, his case studies show the use of local religion and kinship metaphors.

42. "Biejing Residents Protest Against Garbage Dump," *China News Digest*, 11 July, 1997 (GL97–098).

43. "Protestors Clash with Police in Sichuan," *China News Digest*, 15 October 1997 (GL97–141).

44. See Wang, "Mutual Empowerment of State and Peasantry," p. 1435. Li and O'Brien, "Villagers and Popular Resistance," pp. 48–49 also give several examples of rural protest over violations of the election law.

45. See Kelliher, *Peasant Power in China*, and Bernstein, "Incorporating Group Interests," pp. 13–14.

7

Alternate Civilities and
Political Change

This book is part of a growing literature on how civil associations can foster both market success and political change. I have also argued, however, that much of this literature—especially writings on civil society—focuses too much on formally organized and voluntary institutions, and too little on informal associations rooted in community life. This bias reflects the Enlightenment origins of the concept of civil society, and of twentieth-century thinking on modernity more generally. It was the Enlightenment that taught us to look for autonomous individuals reaching their own moral decisions apart from earlier communal moralities, and shifted our attention to what Max Weber would later call the transition from traditional to rational political and economic systems. This image of autonomous individuals also lies at the roots of Habermas's public sphere of critical thinkers and of the idealized version of civil society as a rationalized institution where such individuals can pursue their common interests.

Even in the West this image always described a project more than a consistent social reality. Outside North America and Western Europe it can simply fail to capture how individual identity comes into being, and how identity shapes the creation of broader social groups. These identities, at least in China, have hardly been immune from the Enlightenment project, which entered China in force (and to an extent by force) in the nineteenth century. Yet they still maintain strong links to the bonds of local community, kinship, and religion that too many earlier analysts dismissed as premodern, and that too many recent ones downplay in their search for civil society.

Broadening the scope to include drinking buddies as well as chambers of commerce, or self-interested ghost worshippers as well as organized religious charities, clarifies how these ties continue to be important in building democratic civilities. In particular, it directs our attention to several points that can otherwise be hard to see: how informal associations have survived the buffeting of modernity in both its socialist and capitalist forms; the important but often crucial role of women in such ties; and above all the way these organizations can lay the groundwork for successful political change. Let me conclude by briefly taking up some of these themes that have run through most of the book so far.

The Bifurcation of Social Associations

Theories of modernity, including both its socialist and capitalist variants, conjure up a double threat to social organizations below the state. From below, they argue that a newly autonomous and mobile individual challenges and ultimately dismantles earlier communal moralities and solidarities that had once been taken for granted. This can be seen across a huge swath of human life. It lies behind the Protestant's unmediated, individual relationship to God. It also lurks behind the shrinking role of kinship, as many basic family functions move into the market—food preparation, child care, and now occasionally even pregnancy can be contracted out. The threat from above is the expanding state, which more than fills the void left by decreasing communal ties, enlivened by its new social and technological processes of control. Totalitarian theory describes this dual threat in its extreme form—completely atomized individuals who are therefore powerless to resist an omnipotent state—but no modern society is immune.

On the other hand, the evidence from China and Taiwan shows that the real pressures from these twin threats never fully succeed in wiping out intermediate social organizations. This finding is particularly important given the political history of both places during the twentieth century. Until the democratization of Taiwan during the last decade, they jointly provided a primer on the permutations of authoritarian control. Taiwan tended toward corporatism and relatively free markets, and the People's Republic (until recently) favored mass organizations and central planning. Both, however, encouraged a society of individuals under a powerful state that dictated their moral codes and social lives. And both tried to repress or swallow anything socially intermediate and independent.

Yet ultimately neither one succeeded in this project. The strongest evidence for this is the abundance of civic associations that formed almost overnight in Taiwan after martial law was lifted. That remarkable phenomenon implied that some kind of associational life must have been there all along. We can now see the roots of Taiwan's current vibrant associational world in the uses of personal connections in business, the growth of new religious forms, and the disorganized beginnings of the environmental and other social movements in ties of village, kinship, and temple.

The long history of gaps and openings in political/personal control in the People's Republic equally suggests the impossibility of total control there in practice, as I discussed in Chapter 3. Even during the Cultural Revolution, we saw the continuing importance of kinship, the second economy, and the use of personalistic ties. The move toward a more corporatist model in recent years has further encouraged such ties.

Many of the social ties that continued through the worst abuses of authoritarian control in both the People's Republic and Taiwan are the kinds of things that theorists of modernization had dismissed as "traditional" and thus ultimately doomed—religion, family, and other ties of community over rationality. They were wrong. The empirical evidence from around the world at the close of the twentieth century has largely falsified predictions of the end of the family, the secularization of religion, and the total rationalization of economic ties.

I am not arguing that either market economies or authoritarian control are irrelevant. Markets have in fact encouraged autonomous individualism and undercut many earlier kinds of ties. Repressive governments have pushed hard to eliminate the space for independent social organization. China has been very successful at this, as was Taiwan until the 1980s. The legacy of these pressures in both places, however, has been a bifurcation in the types of civil association, not a destruction of them. Authoritarian rule in both places meant that social capital would have to live primarily in the informal sector, because formally organized associations were either banned or swallowed whole. When more formally organized independent groups were permitted—which has happened to a great extent in Taiwan over the last decade, and is at least nominally beginning in China—they often exist across a great gulf from the informal sector. The formal associations generally do not draw on the sets of semi-communal ties that characterize the informal social sector, as I discussed in the last chapter. For the business, religious, and environmental groups I have been discussing, the result has been one set of national, voluntary associations with close ties to the state, and another set of variable, local, and informally organized ties.

The informal sector, which has lasted through all the struggles and pressures of the twentieth century, holds the embryonic promise of future political changes. More broadly, it suggests that a diversity of opinion and organization, within culturally accepted limits, provides a crucial resource for any society facing major social changes. At least in China and Taiwan, however, this level of organization is also strongly localist, making it difficult to push directly for change, and difficult to organize on a national scale. The formal sector, with its universalizing ideologies and national organization, unites broader groups more easily. Yet it is also too easy to repress or co-opt, as we have seen in the conservatism of most of the big business and religious groups. The real possibilities of alternate social worlds, the seeds of future political organization, lie in the sets of ties that thrive in the informal sector. They remain difficult to mobilize widely under authoritarian rule, but they hold a true potential for change.

Alternate Civilities, Alternate Modernities

I have spared readers further use of the "ancient curse" and "Etch-a-Sketch" metaphors for how culture works that I developed in the first chapter. The substance of what I have been saying, however, illustrates the inadequacy of either extreme to describe how cultural values relate to economic and political change. Each sector examined here shows powerful external forces that are changing Chinese and Taiwanese culture in fundamental ways. Market economies everywhere have led to a rise in individualism, a transformation of many social values to commodities (old age care, for instance), and a general feeling that shared core values—from religion to family—have disappeared as everything opens to critical scrutiny. We have seen this in the increased concern in both China and Taiwan over rising individualism and greed, or in the celebration of just those new values in the ghost cults that swept over Taiwan in the 1980s. At the same time, there is also a strong and direct cultural influence from the West, which has shown up in a range of associations and discourses from the Rotary Club to NGOs, and even in the way nature must be conceived to create an environmental movement like Taiwan's.[1]

Yet earlier values do not just disappear under this onslaught. Cultural values shape how these new influences are understood, and what kinds of responses are possible. Cultures change in this process, but so do market economies and Western ideologies. In business we have seen this in the network capitalism which is so central to how the market has developed in all Chinese societies, and which accounts for both its particular strengths and its weaknesses. In religion it appears in the remarkable blossoming of popular ritual in the People's Republic after so many decades of tight control, and in Taiwan's rapid upsurge and reworking of Buddhism. In the environment it shows up most clearly in the ways that local religion and kinship influence both the organization and the ideology of protest in Taiwan. None of these are simply stubborn survivals of "premodern" life, along the lines of ancient cultural curses. They are instead parts of a uniquely Chinese modernity, its own unique adaptation to markets and new cultural pressures from abroad.

Modernity is a set of very real shared pressures created by the pre-dominance of market logic and, for most of the world today, the power of a global culture with roots in the Western Enlightenment. Those pressures, however, are assimilated, managed, and transformed according to local cultural and social resources. This accounts for the cross-cultural variation in modernity, and also means that modernity takes on different faces even within a single social context. Modernity as really lived, as opposed to the philosophical project of modernity, has everywhere included both the push toward autonomous individuals meeting in the market and reactions against it. Romantics, communists, deep ecologists, and even postmodernists are as central to living modernity in the West as Enlightenment philosophers, neoclassical economists, and Bauhaus architects. Many of the fundamental pressures are the same in China and Taiwan, but the reactions take place on a different ground, and the systems thus evolve differently. We have seen the tension played out here in the attempt to claim a Confucian basis for business success, in the implicit argument between worshipping ghosts for profit and joining Buddhist groups for philanthropy, and in the gap between national NGOs and grassroots movements.

Many now accept the argument that there are alternate economic modernities—that Japanese and Chinese overseas capitalisms do not simply reiterate the Western pattern.[2] The idea that there could be alternate democratic civilities, however, has seen a great deal less attention. The fit between Chinese culture and "civil society" in its usual senses is awkward. In cases where state and society are not thought about as separate entities in tension with each other, the term is difficult to apply. This includes all Chinese states, with the exception of Taiwan since the 1980s and arguably Hong Kong. Civil society is usually also associated with voluntary choices of autonomous individuals, rather than preexisting community ties of various sorts. Many of the groups discussed here, however, rest on a more social logic, from the personal networks of businessmen to the local temple ties of Taiwanese environmental activists.

These difficulties speak less to the inadequacies of Chinese culture in the modern world than to the inadequacies of the concept of civil society. The cultural and social resources of China and Taiwan have a great potential to adapt and contribute to the modern world, including the promotion of thriving civil organizations between family and state. Taiwan in particular shows that it is possible to mobilize a genuine democratic civility on Chinese cultural resources. Some of this clearly grows out of direct contact with the West. The currency of the very idea of "civil society," which is as important now in Taiwan as in Eastern Europe, is a twentieth-century borrowing, as are many of its institutions, from the Rotary Club to Taiwan Greenpeace. International pressures also had some influence on Taiwan's democratization, of course. The fall of Marcos and the large-scale unrest in South Korea in the mid-1980s offered the authoritarian government examples of the dangers of staying the course.[3] Taiwan must also have understood the political capital it would gain in the West from its reforms (as has in fact occurred).

On the other hand, neither international pressure nor direct borrowing from the West explain why the reforms have taken such root internally— why, for example, so many kinds of horizontal associations flowered in the months immediately after martial law was lifted, or why new kinds of large-scale association like Compassionate Relief currently thrive. While some forms of association have been borrowed, the social ties on which they rest have clear Taiwanese and generally Chinese roots. The religious movements build directly on indigenous tradition, and grass-roots environmental action also depends on local social capital, especially organized through religion, kinship, and political factions. These ties may not have had any earlier links to a concept of civil society or to a democratic political culture, but they can be mobilized, just as they have been mobilized in the construction of Taiwan's economic boom.

Women's Leading Roles

As I explored the various sides of local association, a clear gender pattern came into focus: women consistently take leading roles in the informal sector, pushing at the boundaries of local association, and creating the armature of potential political changes.[4] They are at least as important as their husbands in forming social capital. We have seen this in their management of the majority of rotating credit associations, which are themselves a kind of conversion of social to financial capital. It shows up equally in their large share of small, entrepreneurial businesses, the sector most closely tied to informal and semicommunal social ties. The same kinds of effects show up in religion in two different ways, both striking. First, there is the rapid development of female spirit mediums in China; this is an area that women did not always dominate, but where they have been able to move into territory where men see too much political risk. Second, Taiwan's Compassionate Relief Merit Association shows how women can translate what were seen as fundamentally domestic concerns onto a public national (and even international) stage. Women are also mainstays of social movements like the environmental movement. Both China and Taiwan now have environmental NGOs whose members are primarily women, and whose work is characterized by grassroots efforts at relatively apolitical goals like recycling or environmental education. Men's groups, in contrast, tend to be farther from day-to-day household interests, and more concerned with philosophical issues and with crises that require political action.[5]

These roles rarely translate directly into standard political power, although they have led to some important groups in the formal sector that appeal primarily to women, like Taiwan's Compassionate Relief or China's Global Village Beijing. These groups, however, form only a small part of the formal sector, which remains dominated by men. One of the contributions of looking at informal realizations of social capital is the way it clarifies the roles that women are in fact playing locally.

The literature on democratization has not had much to say about women, partly because much of it concentrates on political elites, and partly because it recognizes that social movements, in which women are often active around the world, are no guarantees of democratization. Yet as Georgina Waylen argues in an important article, women have been influential local actors in democratic transitions.[6] The most obvious are the mothers' groups who drew such clear attention to human rights abuses in Chile and Argentina in the 1970s. Women's influence in Latin American transitions was in fact far greater than this, extending to consumption issues and feminism, as well as to social issues. Even Waylen's discussion, however, is limited primarily to the most public roles that women play. The broader look at social capital formation and civil association here encourages a focus on a range of less openly political activities, from business connections to religious networks built around spirit mediumship.

Like the analysis here, Waylen points to women's political weakness as one of the keys to their strength in the informal sector. She points out that military regimes in Latin America often did not see women's activities as dangerous enough to warrant repression. In addition, the most effective public protests (like the Madres' human rights protests) hinged on women's claims of traditional roles as wife and mother, which made them more difficult to persecute. The closure of public political space by these authoritarian regimes in Latin America moved activity into the informal sector and inadvertently strengthened the role of women.[7] Women's roles in civil associations in China and Taiwan stem from just these processes, although the details of the regimes and of women's actions are quite different from the Latin American cases.

For the East European transitions, however, Waylen concludes that women remained largely on the sidelines. She argues that after decades of enforced women's liberation from above, where women were usually obliged to work in emulation of muscular socialist-realist models, "the family and home were often seen as a haven from the demands and interference of the state and a site of resistance, a place of autonomy and creativity in the absence of a full-fledged civil society."[8] China also valorized women at work (while paying them less than their husbands), and also granted them rights by fiat from above. Yet women there are not so clearly on the sidelines, and not so clearly different from their cousins in Taiwan.

Chinese women have undoubtedly "feminized" to an extent since the reforms began to open up personal space two decades ago. Many curl their hair and gravitate to lacy clothing and shiny shoes. Yet they have not fled into the home, and in many cases lead the way in creating new kinds of horizontal ties. In very different ways, women spirit mediums, participants in rotating credit associations, or organizers of volunteer environmental action have pushed to create new social capital ahead of their more conservative husbands. In part, this appears different from Waylen's description of Eastern Europe because nearly all of it occurs in the informal and semicommunal sector, which (like most analysts) she downplays. It may also be occurring because the transition in China has been so gradual and partial compared to the Eastern European cases. Chinese women have already had twenty years to play out their reaction to official socialist feminism.

Can women's important roles in creating informal social organizations survive a democratic transition? Their ability to succeed at this in authoritarian situations depended in part on their greater free space compared to men, who were more closely under state control. As democratization eases controls on men, and as informal social ties can move into the formal sector, one might predict that men take over leadership roles. The evidence from Taiwan is mixed on this. Men clearly control the major political and economic organizations, and much of the NGO sector. On the other hand, women remain important in informal ties (religion, rotating credit associations) and now, for the first time, dominate in some formal associations like Compassionate Relief or the Homemakers' Union. These are long-term transformations in women's positions with roots in the informal ties they cemented during the authoritarian period. Any democratic transition in China, of course, is still a matter of speculation, but women's activities are increasing the chances that such a change would be successful by establishing the kinds of ties that will be needed.

Associational Life and Political Transformations

Taiwan now has a civil society in the usual senses of the term. This is a statement that neither I nor nearly any other observer would have predicted two decades ago as we watched yet another wave of dissidents being sentenced to long prison terms. This transformation speaks to the possibilities of Chinese culture, at least in Taiwan's particular social context. China may never have had a democratic political culture, but it did have the kinds of intermediate institutions outside politics that could evolve to support one. The Taiwan case thus requires a revision of the most pessimistic arguments about the PRC, and provides a challenge to Singapore's claim to speak for the naturalness of Chinese authoritarian culture.

Is there a "Taiwan model" for the transition to democratic civility that China or other places could follow? The short answer is no: Taiwan's history and current political conundrums make it unique. After all, this would be the third generation of Taiwan models, none of which turned out to generalize very well. The first was Taiwan's Land to the Tiller program, the land reform program of the early 1950s that so successfully eliminated the large landholding class in favor of independent small farmers. This is the goal most land reforms fail to achieve, including those (like South Vietnam in the 1960s) that emulated Taiwan. Taiwan's political situation at the time was unique. As a powerful and largely external force, the Nationalist government could afford to alienate the local elite; in addition, the combination of United States aid and state-owned assets left over from Japanese rule made it possible to buy landlords out. The second potential model is Taiwan's rapid economic growth, especially in the 1970s. Here again, however, unique features like Taiwan's cultural endowment and the timing of its entry into the world market system could not simply be reproduced at will elsewhere.[9]

By rooting Taiwan's democratic transition in its specific social and historical context I have also meant to discourage any blind emulation of still another model. Yet Taiwan does offer us important lessons about how and when social associations can foster democratic civility. It reminds us how horizontal ties of social trust can survive an authoritarian state, especially as informal associations. These associations provide small reservoirs of social capital that can multiply when political situations change. They also maintained a certain pressure within Taiwan's authoritarian system, a kind of counterbalance to the power of the state. The wealth of these informal ties explains why Taiwan's formal civil sector developed with such extraordinary speed after martial law was lifted.

Taiwan also reminds us, however, that social organizations do not automatically lead to democratization, and that corporatist arrangements like the one Taiwan had can go on for decades. Such governments certainly do not stamp out horizontal social association, but they can put effective limits on it through a combination of repression and control. This is why, for example, big business was not a major factor pushing for democratic reforms in Taiwan. Social organizations may be necessary to a successful democratic transition, but they are not sufficient. Taiwan's metamorphosis to democratic civility has roots in at least two additional areas: a cultural ideal of civility, and a central government that finally agreed to incorporate its social organizations in a new way.

China shares a great deal of this legacy with Taiwan, although a half-century of Japanese colonialism in Taiwan and another half-century of socialism in China have helped differentiate them from each other. Both, for example, share a long cultural emphasis on the idea of civility/civilization. In spite of the association between ideals of civility and civil society in the West, however, this is no guarantee of democracy. Civil society may indeed require some degree of civility—a minimal ability to accept the "otherness" of others, at least within mutually expected boundaries. Yet the reverse is clearly not necessary: civility can play a central role and not offer an iota of pressure toward building a civil society. The primary Chinese use of "civility" in this century (under both Republican and Communist rule) has been as a prop for authoritarian rule. The Communists in particular tried to colonize the entire society from the state, and campaigns for polite behavior are a small part of that larger effort (see Chapter 2).

China has an equally long history of horizontal associations. Taiwan showed how these can aid the development of a genuine civil society even though they were rather different from the Western tradition. The significance of much of this is missed in China because analysts have tended to concentrate on the formal civil sector of NGOs, which is both very limited and closely tied to the state in China. The more important social ties for China's future development are the myriad of small-scale and local groups that permeate the country, from earth god temple groups to periodic dinners that bring together business friends. These groups look less modern, and less like Western civil society—they are local, informal, and membership is often partially communal. The government also effectively keeps these groups small and relatively disorganized. Yet they are a key to a rapid and successful civil transformation, just as they were in Taiwan.

Taiwan's experience differed from most of Chinese history in two critical ways: its success in the market economy, and the eventual decision of its political elite to step back from attempts at total social control. The People's Republic of China has increasingly opened to market forces, but the political elite so far shows no interest in the diversity of a civil society. Neither social capital in the form of horizontal associations nor a shared moral consensus around the idea of civility suffices by itself to create a civil society. As the preceding chapters have shown, a solidly entrenched authoritarian state can successfully limit and co-opt these forces for many decades.

This will appear as bad news to those who look for an instantaneous transformation of China into a Western-style democracy. The forms of civil association I have documented do not necessarily imply a political conversion. Yet this is a limiting view. In the present these associations are helping to reconstruct a social world that is not simply an extension of the state. That is, they mark a significant departure from the old totalitarian project of microscopic control over every aspect of life. These newly created or revived organizations once again provide economic, social, and moral resources to people. In addition, they offer the future possibility of a social base on which to build democracy if the government does change course. Democracies require a certain amount of free space left by the state, but they also require a lively society to step into that space. Without the precursors that are being reborn in China, it would run the risk of emulating some of the worst of the East European experiences, where the lack of social resources either returns Communists to power or allows the meteoric rise of gangsterism and other signs of uncivil society. The Taiwan precedent offers no guarantee of a similarly rapid transition for China, but it does show how a society very like China's can successfully take advantage of opportunities that occur.

This evidence on the importance of small-scale associations suggests certain policy directions, both for China and for countries with a democratic agenda. China has allowed a burgeoning of these groups over the last two decades, but has also suffered periodic bouts of cold feet about them. They have refused to register new groups at some times, or have restricted each sector to only one such group. In part these reactions represent a fear that such groups, left out of control, could indeed instigate a political transformation. In part, they also show a modernist drive to create groups in a single image of voluntary membership and formalized rules of bureaucratic management. The lesson of Taiwan, however, is that small and more traditional-looking groups pose little immediate political threat on their own. In addition, once the government has thrown off the daunting agenda of truly totalitarian control over the minutia of life and thought, such reservoirs of social capital can help to maintain local society as the state steps back. Some of them may rely on older kinds of communal ties like lineage or temple, but in fact they can work well in the modern economy.

For foreign governments and organizations interested in building civil institutions in China, these findings suggest first that we expand our vision beyond the standard NGO sector. These large and formal associations look appropriately modern and similar enough to Western ideas of civil society to have attracted large amounts of international funding and attention. Yet these associations are also closely intertwined with the government in China, even more than had been true earlier in Taiwan. They are registered in government units, and almost always feature current or retired high officials in prominent positions. They may suggest a precedent for some potential future organization that would be nongovernmental, but they are extremely unlikely to act independently of the government under the current system. They do not represent the society to the state, as in the Western view of civil society, but are a continuation of the Chinese and socialist ideal of joining society and state into a single unit.

In addition, these institutions tend to be very distant from actual social ties on the ground. They are urban (mostly Beijing-centered), highly educated groups in a country that is mostly rural and relatively uneducated. Even more than in Taiwan, there is a gulf between these elite organizations and the daily life of most people. This is one reason that membership remains so small, and voluntary participation so marginal for most groups. If, as Robert Putnam argues, social capital is the key to making democracy work, then for China it lies much more in the thick social ties of the informal sector than in formally arranged NGOs, more in local initiative than in organization from above or abroad.[10]

The resources embedded in these local civil associations also have implications for the discourse on human rights. Much of the international criticism of human rights concentrates on political freedoms, which are indeed severely curtailed in China. China's response, in part, has been to assert a broader notion of rights, and to point to increases in personal and economic freedoms. Those changes are real, and the Taiwan experience suggests that critics should take them more seriously. China has allowed an enormous amount of free space to open up in the last few years. I have argued that even attempts at strong totalitarian control leave some inevitable but unintentional free space for personal and social ties. China, however, has purposely backed away from many aspects of totalitarian social control over the last two decades. Much of the current free space is now intentional, and that constitutes a radical change of attitude by the government. Political openness was the very last step in Taiwan's transition, but the success of that transition depended on a social world that had grown up in the preceding decades. China is only just starting on this path, and it will be important to encourage it to walk more boldly through the door it has already opened.

Denunciations of political imprisonments and threats of trade sanctions may be important as ways of claiming a moral position, but they have hardly induced China to undertake serious political reform. If China undergoes a political change like Taiwan's, its success will rely much more on an increase in the legal space created for a social world beyond the state, and on having the social resources to fill that space. China has moved strongly in that direction, and can be encouraged to go further especially through the economy. World Trade Organization membership or pressure from international investors to create legal guarantees for their businesses are the sorts of things that will encourage China to consolidate these kinds of changes out of self-interest. Trade sanctions, on the other hand, strike against exactly the sector that has most encouraged the development of new civil associations.

This is a gradualist formula for political change that will not please those who dream of an immediate transformation. But there is no reason to think that shock therapy will work any better in politics than it has in economics. China is just beginning to create the social resources it will need for a successful alternate democratic civility.

Notes

1. See Robert P. Weller and Peter K. Bol, "From Heaven-and-Earth to Nature: Chinese Concepts of the Environment and Their Influence on Policy Implementation," in Mary Evelyn Tucker and John Berthrong, eds., *Confucianism and Ecology: The Interrelation of Heaven, Earth, and Humans* (Cambridge, Mass.: Harvard University Center for the Study of World Religions, 1998), pp. 313–341, for more on the development of the idea of "nature" in twentieth-century China.

2. The recent Asian economic problems have led some to declare the death of Asian alternatives, but this ignores the influence the "Asian" model has already had on Western practice, as well as being premature.

3. Chiang Ching-kuo's apparent change of heart about how Taiwan should be run in the last years of his life—unexpected by most observers and still not fully explained—also set the stage for the reforms.

4. I am especially grateful to the Taiwanese sociologist Chang Wei-an on this point. He first forced my attention to the pattern developing in what were then a scattered set of draft papers.

5. The active and early involvement of women in social movements goes back earlier in twentieth-century China, for instance with the early organization of women against foot-binding in Shanghai. See Tang Zhenchang, "Civil Consciousness and Shanghai Society," *Social Sciences in China* (Spring 1995), 58–73.

6. Waylen, "Women and Democratization."

7. Ibid., pp. 338–339.

8. Ibid., p. 345.

9. See Hsin-Huang Michael Hsiao, "An East Asian Development Model: Empirical Explorations," in Peter L. Berger and Hsin-Huang Michael Hsiao, eds., *In Search of an East Asian Development Model* (New Brunswick: Transaction, 1988), pp. 12–23.

10. Putnam, *Making Democracy Work*, p. 185.

Appendix
Chinese Character List

Note: All terms are Mandarin Chinese, romanized in pinyin, and written in simplified characters, unless otherwise noted.

chujia	出家
Cicheng Dui	慈承队
Ciji Gongdehui	慈济功德会
cunmin weiyuanhui	村民委员会
danwei	单位
fangsheng hui	放生会
fa lu	发炉
fanying	反映
faren	法人
fenxiang	分香
ge shen	革身
geti hu	个体户
gong	公
gong fei	共匪
gongmin shehui	公民社会
guan	官
guanxi	关係
huat lo (Hokkien)	发炉
jianju	检举
jiao	醮

jiedao weiyuanhui	街道委员会
Jinghua	净化
li	礼
Li Bu	礼部
liuxu	溜须
minjian shehui	民间社会
neiren	内人
Ong Ia (Hokkien)	王爷
poe (Hokkien)	杯
Pudu	普度
qi	气
qigong	气功
Qingshui Zushi Gong	清水祖师公
Qu Yuan	屈原
Raozhi	绕止
renhe	人和
renqing	人情
shangyou	上油
shanshu	善书
shetan	社坛
shimin shehui	市民社会
si	私
siying qiye	私营企业
Songjiang Zhen	松江阵
sunzi	孙子
tong	同
tong xiang	同乡
tongxiang hui	同乡会

tong xing	同姓
tongxing hui	同姓会
tong xue	同学
tudi gong	土地公
tudi miao	土地庙
wen	文
wenhua	文化
wenming	文明
wenming shehui	文明社会
wenya	文雅
wu	武
xian	仙
xiangtu wenxue	乡土文学
xietiao hui	协调会
xinling huanjing	心灵环境
xinyong	信用
Yiguan Dao	一贯道
you	友
yuan	缘
zhai tang	斋堂
zisun	子孙

Bibliography

Anagnost, Ann S. 1997. *National Past-times: Narrative, Writing, and History in Modern China*. Durham, N.C.: Duke University Press.

_____. 1987. "Politics and Magic in Contemporary China." *Modern China* 13(1):40–61.

Arendt, Hannah. 1958. *The Origins of Totalitarianism*. 2d ed. Cleveland: World Publishing Company, Meridian.

Baptandier, Brigitte. 1996. "The Lady Linshui: How a Woman Became a Goddess." In Meir Shahar and Robert P. Weller, eds., *Unruly Gods: Divinity and Society in China*, 105–49. Honolulu, Hawaii: University of Hawaii Press.

Bell, Lynda S. 1994. "For Better, for Worse: Women and the World Market in Rural China." *Modern China* 20(2):180–210.

Bellah, Robert N. 1965. "Epilogue: Religion and Progress in Modern Asia." In Robert N. Bellah, ed., *Religion and Progress in Modern Asia*, 168–229. New York: Free Press.

Berger, Peter, Brigitte Berger, and Hansfried Kellner. 1973. *The Homeless Mind: Modernization and Consciousness*. New York: Vintage.

Berling, Judith A. 1985. "Religion and Popular Culture: The Management of Moral Capital in *The Romance of the Three Teachings*." In David Johnson, Andrew J. Nathan, and Evelyn S. Rawski, eds., *Popular Culture in Late Imperial China*, 188–218. Berkeley: University of California Press.

Bernstein, Richard, and Ross H. Munro. 1997. *The Coming Conflict with China*. New York: Knopf.

Bernstein, Thomas P. 1996. "Incorporating Group Interests Into the Policy Process: The Case of Farmers During the Reform Era." Paper Presented to the Conference on "The Non-Economic Impact of China's Economic Reforms." Harvard University.

Boddy, Janice. 1989. *Wombs and Alien Spirits: Women, Men, and the Zar Cult in Northern Sudan*. Madison, Wisc.: University of Wisconsin Press.

Bol, Peter K. 1993. "Government, Society, and State: On the Political Visions of Ssu-ma Kuang and Wang An-shih." In Robert P. Hymes and Conrad Schirokauer, eds., *Ordering the World: Approaches to State and Society in Sung Dynasty China*, 128–192. Berkeley: University of California Press.

Bosco, Joseph. 1992. "Taiwan Factions: *Guanxi*, Patronage and the State in Local Politics." *Ethnology* 31(2):157–183.

_____. 1994. "Family Factories in Taiwan: The Use and Abuse of the Family Metaphor." Paper Presented at the Annual Meeting of the American Anthropological Association. Atlanta.

Brook, Timothy. 1993. *Praying for Power: Buddhism and the Formation of Gentry Society in Late-Ming China.* Cambridge, Mass.: Harvard-Yenching Institute.

――――. 1997. "Auto-organization in Chinese Society." In Timothy Brook and B. Michael Frolic, eds., *Civil Society in China*, 19–45. Armonk, N.Y.: M. E. Sharpe.

Buchowski, Michal. 1996. "The Shifting Meanings of Civil and Civic Society in Poland." In Chris Hann and Elizabeth Dunn, eds., *Civil Society: Challenging Western Notions*, 79–98. London: Routledge.

Chamberlain, Heath B. 1993. "On the Search for Civil Society in China." *Modern China* 19(2):199–215.

Chan, Anita, Richard Madsen, and Jonathan Unger. 1992. *Chen Village Under Mao and Deng.* 2d ed. Berkeley: University of California Press.

Chan, Kin-man, and Haixiong Qiu. 1998. "Small Government, Big Society: Social Organizations and Civil Society in China." *China Area Studies Series* (Japan) 8:34–47.

Chan, Wing-tsit, comp. 1963. *A Source Book in Chinese Philosophy.* Princeton: Princeton University Press.

Chance, Norman A. 1991. *China's Urban Villagers: Changing Life in a Beijing Suburb.* 2d ed. Fort Worth, Tex.: Holt, Rinehart and Winston.

Chang, Hao. 1996. "The Intellectual Heritage of the Confucian Ideal of *Ching-shih*." In Wei-ming Tu, ed., *Confucian Traditions in East Asian Modernity*, 72–91. Cambridge, Mass.: Harvard University Press.

Chen, Nancy. 1994. "Mystics, Millenarians and *Mixin*." Paper Presented at the Association for Asian Studies. Boston.

Ciji Gongdehui. n.d. "Wuyuan Daci Tongti Dabei [Great Beneficence to Known and Unknown, and Boundless Compassion for All]." Brochure. n.p.

Clunas, Craig. 1996. *Fruitful Sites: Garden Culture in Ming Dynasty China.* Durham, N.C.: Duke University Press.

Cohen, Myron L. 1990. "Lineage Organization in North China." *Journal of Asian Studies* 49(3):509–534.

Dasgupta, Susmita, and David Wheeler. 1996. *Citizen Complaints as Environmental Indicators: Evidence from China.* Report to PRDEI, World Bank.

de Bary, William Theodore. 1996. "Confucian Education in Premodern East Asia." In Wei-ming Tu, ed., *Confucian Traditions in East Asian Modernity*, 21–37. Cambridge: Harvard University Press.

de Tocqueville, Alexis. 1954[1945]. *Democracy in America.* Rev. ed. Vol. 1. Eds. Francis Bowen and Phillips Bradley. New York: Vintage.

Dean, Kenneth. 1993. *Taoist Ritual and Popular Cults of Southeast China.* Princeton: Princeton University Press.

――――. 1997. "Ritual and Space: Civil Society or Popular Religion?" In Timothy Brook and B. Michael Frolic, eds., *Civil Society in China*, 172–192. Armonk, N.Y.: M. E. Sharpe.

Dirlik, Arif. 1975. "The Ideological Foundations of the New Life Movement: A Study in Counterrevolution." *Journal of Asian Studies* 34(4):945–80.

Duara, Prasenjit. 1988a. *Culture, Power, and the State: Rural North China, 1900–1942.* Stanford: Stanford University Press.

――――. 1988b. "Superscribing Symbols: The Myth of Guandi, Chinese God of War." *Journal of Asian Studies* 47(4):778–795.

_____. 1991. "Knowledge and Power in the Discourse of Modernity: The Campaigns Against Popular Religion in Early Twentieth-century China." *Journal of Asian Studies* 50(1):67–83.

Ebrey, Patricia Buckley, trans. 1991a. *Chu Hsi's Family Rituals: A Twelfth-Century Chinese Manual for the Performance of Cappings, Weddings, Funerals, and Ancestral Rites.* Princeton: Princeton University Press.

_____. 1991b. *Confucianism and Family Rituals in Imperial China: A Social History of Writing About Rites.* Princeton: Princeton University Press.

Forney, Matt. 1998. "Voice of the People." *Far Eastern Economic Review* (May 7):10–12.

Foucault, Michel. 1979. *Discipline and Punish: The Birth of the Prison.* Trans. Alan Sheridan. New York: Random House, Vintage.

Freedman, Maurice. 1959. "The Handling of Money: A Note on the Background to the Economic Sophistication of Overseas Chinese." *Man* 59:64–65.

Fukuyama, Francis. 1989. "The End of History?" *The National Interest* 16 (Summer):3–18.

_____. 1995. *Trust: Social Virtues and the Creation of Prosperity.* New York: Free Press.

Gábor, István R. 1991. "Modernity or a New Kind of Duality? Second Thoughts on the 'Second Economy.'" Paper presented at the Conference on the Obstacles to the Transformation of Soviet-type Societies in Eastern Europe. Vienna. photocopy.

Gardella, Robert. 1992. "Squaring Accounts: Commercial Bookkeeping Methods and Capitalist Rationalism in Late Qing and Republican China." *Journal of Asian Studies* 51(2):317–339.

Gates, Hill. 1991. "'Narrow Hearts' and Petty Capitalism: Small Business Women in Chengdu, China." In Alice Littlefield and Hill Gates, eds., *Marxist Approaches in Economic Anthropology,* 13–36. Lanham, Md.: University Press of America.

Gold, Thomas B. 1985. "After Comradeship: Personal Relations in China Since the Cultural Revolution." *China Quarterly* 104 (December):657–675.

_____. 1996. "Civil Society in Taiwan: The Confucian Dimension." In Wei-ming Tu, ed., *Confucian Traditions in East Asian Modernity,* 244–258. Cambridge, Mass.: Harvard University Press.

Granovetter, Mark. 1985. "Economic Action and Social Structure: The Problem of Embeddedness." *American Journal of Sociology* 91(3):481–510.

Grove, Richard. 1993. "Conserving Eden: The (European) East India Companies and Their Environmental Policies on St. Helena, Mauritius, and in Western India, 1660–1854." *Comparative Studies in Society and History* 35(2):318–351.

Gu, Edward X. 1998. "'Non-Establishment' Intellectuals, Public Space, and the Creation of Non-governmental Organizations in China: The Chen Ziming-Wang Juntao Saga." *China Journal* (39):39–58.

Hamilton, Gary G. 1998. "Culture and Organization in Taiwan's Market Economy." In Robert W. Hefner, ed., *Market Cultures: Society and Morality in the New Asian Capitalisms,* 41–77. Boulder: Westview Press.

Handlin, Joanna F. 1975. "Lü Kun's New Audience: The Influence of Women's Literacy on Sixteenth-century Thought." In Margery Wolf and Roxane Witke, eds., *Women in Chinese Society*, 13–38. Stanford: Stanford University Press.

Hann, Chris. 1996. "Introduction: Political Society and Civil Anthropology." In Chris Hann and Elizabeth Dunn, eds., *Civil Society: Challenging Western Models*, 1–26. London: Routledge.

Hann, Chris, and Elizabeth Dunn, eds. 1996. *Civil Society: Challenging Western Models*. London: Routledge.

Harrell, Stevan. 1985. "Why Do the Chinese Work So Hard?" *Modern China* 11(2):203–226.

Hefner, Robert W. 1998a. "From Civil Society to Democratic Civility." In Robert W. Hefner, ed., *Democratic Civility: The History and Cross-cultural Possibility of a Modern Ideal*. New Brunswick, N.J.: Transaction.

_____. 1998b. "A Muslim Civil Society? Indonesian Reflections on the Conditions of Its Possibility." In Robert W. Hefner, ed., *Democratic Civility: The History and Cross-cultural Possibility of a Modern Ideal*. New Brunswick, N.J.: Transaction.

Hertz, Ellen. 1998. *The Trading Crowd: An Ethnography of the Shanghai Stock Market*. Cambridge: Cambridge University Press.

Hsiao, Hsin-Huang Michael. 1988a. *Qishi Niandai Fan Wuran Zili Jiuji de Jiegou yu Guocheng Fenxi [Analysis of the Structure and Process of Anti-pollution Self-help Movements in the 1980s]*. Taipei: Xingzheng Yuan Huanjing Baohu.

_____. 1988b. *The Nonprofit Sector in Taiwan: Current State, New Trends and Future Prospects*. Report to the Asia Pacific Philanthropy Consortium, NGO Sector Preparatory Meeting. Bangkok.

_____. 1988c. "An East Asian Development Model: Empirical Explorations." In Peter L. Berger and Hsin-Huang Michael Hsiao, eds., *In Search of an East Asian Development Model*, 12–23. New Brunswick: Transaction.

_____. 1995. "The State and Business Relations in Taiwan." *Journal of Far Eastern Business* 1(3):76–97.

Hsiao, Hsin-Huang Michael, Lester W. Milbrath, and Robert P. Weller. 1995. "Antecedents of an Environmental Movement in Taiwan." *Capitalism, Nature, Socialism* 6(3):91–104.

Huang, Chien-yu Julia, and Robert P. Weller. 1998. "Merit and Mothering: Women and Social Welfare in Taiwanese Buddhism." *Journal of Asian Studies* 57(2):379–396.

Huang, Shu-min. 1989. *The Spiral Road: Changes in a Chinese Village Through the Eyes of a Communist Party Leader*. Boulder: Westview Press.

Huang Chün-chieh and Wu Kuang-ming. 1994. "Taiwan and the Confucian Aspiration: Toward the Twenty-first Century." In Stevan Harrell and Huang Chün-chieh, eds., *Cultural Change in Postwar Taiwan*, 69–87. Boulder: Westview Press.

Huang Guangguo. 1984. "Rujia Lunli yu Qiye Zuzhi Xingtai [Confucian Theory and Types of Enterprise Organization]." In *Zhongguoshi Guanli [Chinese Style Management]*, 21–58. Taipei: Gongshang Shibao.

Huntington, Samuel P. 1991. *The Third Wave: Democratization in the Late Twentieth Century*. Norman, Okla.: University of Oklahoma Press.

_____. 1996. *The Clash of Civilizations and the Remaking of World Order*. New York: Simon & Schuster.

Hymes, Robert. n.d. *Way and Byway*. Unpublished Manuscript.

Jing, Jun. 1994. "Female Autonomy and Female Shamans in Northwest China." Paper Presented at the Annual Meeting of the American Anthropological Association. Atlanta.

_____. Forthcoming. "Environmental Protests in Rural China." In Mark Selden and Elizabeth Perry, eds., *Social Protests in China*. New York: Routledge.

Jochim, Christian. 1992. "Confucius and Capitalism: Views of Confucianism in Works on Confucianism and Economic Development." *Journal of Chinese Religions* 20:135–171.

Jordan, David K., and Daniel L. Overmyer. 1986. *The Flying Phoenix: Aspects of Chinese Sectarianism in Taiwan*. Princeton: Princeton University Press.

Katz, Paul R. 1995. *Demon Hordes and Burning Boats: The Cult of Marshal Wen in Late Imperial Chekiang*. Albany, N.Y.: State University of New York Press.

Ka Chih-ming. 1992. "Chengxiang Yimin, Xiaoxing Qiye yu Dushi Fei Zhengshi Jingji zhi Xingcheng [Rural Migrants in the City, Small Enterprises and the Formation of the Urban Informal Economy]." Paper presented at the Workshop on Enterprises, Social Relations, and Cultural Practices Studies of Chinese Societies. Taipei.

Kelliher, Daniel. 1992. *Peasant Power in China: The Era of Rural Reform, 1979–1989*. New Haven: Yale University Press.

Kipnis, Andrew B. 1997. *Producing Guanxi: Sentiment, Self, and Subculture in a North China Village*. Durham: Duke University Press.

Ko, Dorothy. 1994. *Teachers of the Inner Chambers: Women and Culture in Seventeenth-century China*. Stanford: Stanford University Press.

Kuo, Eddie C. Y. 1996. "Confucianism as Political Discourse in Singapore: The Case of an Incomplete Revitalization Movement." In Wei-ming Tu, ed., *Confucian Traditions in East Asian Modernity*, 294–309. Cambridge: Harvard University Press.

Lefort, Claude. 1986. *The Political Forms of Modern Society: Bureaucracy, Democracy, Totalitarianism*. Ed. John B. Thompson. Cambridge: MIT Press.

Levy, Marion J., Jr. 1949. *The Family Revolution in Modern China*. Cambridge, Mass.: Harvard University Press.

Lewis, Ioan M. 1971. *Ecstatic Religion: An Anthropological Study of Spirit Possession and Shamanism*. Harmondsworth, England: Penguin.

Li, Jiansheng. 1999. *Changing Kinship Relations and Their Effects on Contemporary Urban Chinese Society*. Ph.D. Dissertation, Boston University.

Li, Lianjiang, and Kevin J. O'Brien. 1996. "Villagers and Popular Resistance in Contemporary China." *Modern China* 22(1):28–61.

Lin Benxuan. 1996. "Zongjiao Yundong de Shehui Jichu—Yi Ciji Gongdehui Wei Lie [The Social Base of a Religious Movement—the Example of the Compassion Merit Society]." Paper presented to the Conference on the Study of Taiwanese Buddhism. National Taiwan University.

Li Yih-yuan. 1992. "Taiwan Minjian Zongjiao de Xiandai Qushi: Dui Peter Berger Jiaoshou Dongya Fazhan Wenhua Yinsu Lun de Huiying [The Modern Tendencies of Taiwan's Popular Religion: A Response to Professor Peter Berger's

Theory of Cultural Factors in East Asian Development]." In *Wenhua de Tuxiang* *[The Image of Culture]*, vol. 2, 117–38. Taipei: Chongchen Wenhua.

Lu Hwei-syin. 1991. "Women's Self-growth Groups and Empowerment of the 'Uterine Family' in Taiwan." *Bulletin of the Institute of Ethnology, Academia Sinica* 71:29–62.

McEwen, Susan. 1994. *Markets, Modernization, and Individualism in Three Chinese Societies.* Ph.D. Dissertation, Boston University.

Mackay, George L. 1895. *From Far Formosa: The Island, Its People and Missions.* 4th ed. New York: Fleming H. Revell.

McKean, Margaret A. 1981. *Environmental Protest and Citizen Politics in Japan.* Berkeley: University of California Press.

MacKenzie, John M. 1988. *The Empire of Nature: Hunting, Conservation and British Imperialism.* Manchester: Manchester University Press.

Malarney, Shaun Kingsley. 1994. "Reconstructing the Public Domain: Changing Women's Roles and the Resurgence of Public Ritual in Contemporary Northern Viet Nam." Paper presented to the annual meeting of the American Anthropological Association. Atlanta.

Mann, Susan. 1997. *Precious Records: Women in China's Long Eighteenth Century.* Stanford: Stanford University Press.

Metzger, Thomas A. 1977. *Escape from Predicament: Neo-Confucianism and China's Evolving Political Culture.* New York: Columbia University Press.

Naquin, Susan. 1992. "The Peking Pilgrimage to Miao-feng Shan: Religious Organizations and Sacred Site." In Susan Naquin and Chün-fang Yü, eds., *Pilgrims and Sacred Sites in China*, 333–377. Berkeley: University of California Press.

Naquin, Susan, and Chün-fang Yü, eds. 1992. *Pilgrims and Sacred Sites in China.* Berkeley: University of California Press.

Nevitt, Christopher Earle. 1996. "Private Business Associations in China: Evidence of Civil Society or State Power?" *China Journal* (36):25–43.

Numazaki, Ichiro. 1991. "The Role of Personal Networks in the Making of Taiwan's *Guanxiqiye* ('Related Enterprises')." In Gary G. Hamilton, ed., *Business Networks and Economic Development in East and Southeast Asia*, 77–93. Hong Kong: Centre of Asian Studies, University of Hong Kong.

Oi, Jean. 1989. *State and Peasant in Contemporary China.* Berkeley: University of California Press.

Osnos, Evan. 1999. *An Analysis of China's Environmental NGOs: Group Involvement in the Emergence of Civil Society.* Senior Honors Thesis, Harvard University.

Polanyi, Karl. 1957. *The Great Transformation.* Intro. by Robert M. MacIver. Boston: Beacon Press.

Putnam, Robert D. 1993. *Making Democracy Work: Civic Traditions in Modern Italy.* Princeton: Princeton University Press.

———. 1995. "Bowling Alone: America's Declining Social Capital." *Journal of Democracy* 6(1):65–78.

Pye, Lucian W. 1988. *The Mandarin and the Cadre: China's Political Cultures.* Ann Arbor, Mich.: Center for Chinese Studies, University of Michigan.

———. 1991. "The State and the Individual: An Overview Interpretation." *China Quarterly* (September):443–66.

_____. 1992 [1968]. *The Spirit of Chinese Politics*. Rev. Ed. Cambridge, Mass.: Harvard University Press.

Qu Haiyuan. 1989. *Minjian Xinyang yu Jingji Fazhan [Popular Beliefs and Economic Development]*. Report to the Taiwan Provincial Government. N.p.: Taiwan Shengzhengfu Minzhengting.

Rankin, Mary Backus. 1993. "Some Observations on a Chinese Public Sphere." *Modern China* 19(2):158–182.

Redding, S. Gordon. 1990. *The Spirit of Chinese Capitalism*. Berlin: Walter de Gruyter.

_____. 1996. "'Thickening' Civil Society: The Impact of Multinationals in China." *Development and Democracy* 11:21–28.

Rigger, Shelley. 1993. "Electoral Strategies and Political Institutions in the Republic of China on Taiwan." Fairbank Center Working Papers, No. 1. Cambridge, Mass.

Rowe, William T. 1993. "The Problem of 'Civil Society' in Late Imperial China." *Modern China* 19(2):139–157.

Sangren, P. Steven. 1979. *A Chinese Marketing Community: An Historical Ethnography of Ta-Ch'i, Taiwan*. Ph.D. Dissertation Stanford University.

_____. 1984. "Traditional Chinese Corporations: Beyond Kinship." *Journal of Asian Studies* 43(3):391–415.

_____. 1987. *History and Magical Power in a Chinese Community*. Stanford: Stanford University Press.

Scott, James C. 1985. *Weapons of the Weak: Everyday Forms of Peasant Resistance*. New Haven: Yale University Press.

Seligman, Adam B. 1992. *The Idea of Civil Society*. New York: Free Press.

"Shenmi Jiaopai Chongshi Tianri [A Secret Sect Sees the Light of Day Again]." 1990. *Yazhou Zhoukan*, 5 August, 28–39.

Shils, Edward. 1996. "Reflections on Civil Society and Civility in the Chinese Intellectual Tradition." In Wei-ming Tu, ed., *Confucian Traditions in East Asian Modernity*, 38–71. Cambridge: Harvard University Press.

Shi Xinmin. 1988. "Fakan Ci [Editor's Introduction]." *Taiwan Huanjing [Taiwan Environment]* 1:1.

Shue, Vivienne. 1988. *The Reach of the State: Sketches of the Chinese Body Politic*. Stanford: Stanford University Press.

Sicular, Terry. 1996. "Redefining State, Plan and Market: China's Reforms in Agricultural Commerce." In Andrew G. Walder, ed., *China's Transitional Economy*, 58–84. New York: Oxford University Press.

Siu, Helen F. 1989. "Recycling Rituals: Politics and Popular Culture in Contemporary Rural China." In Perry Link, Richard Madsen, and Paul Pickowicz, eds., *Unofficial China: Popular Culture and Thought in the People's Republic*, 121–137. Boulder: Westview Press.

Skoggard, Ian A. 1996. *The Indigenous Dynamic in Taiwan's Postwar Development: The Religious and Historical Roots of Entrepreneurship*. Armonk, N.Y.: M. E. Sharpe.

Smith, Joanna F. Handlin. 1987. "Benevolent Societies: The Reshaping of Charity During the Late Ming and Early Ch'ing." *Journal of Asian Studies* 46(2):309–337.

_____. 1992. "Gardens in Ch'i Piao-chia's Social World: Wealth and Values in Late-Ming Kiangnan." *Journal of Asian Studies* 51(1):55–81.

Song Qiang, Zhang Zangzang, Qiao Ben, Gu Qingsheng, and Tang Zhengyu. 1996. *Zhongguo Keyi Shuo Bu: Lengzhan Hou Shidai de Zhengzhi yu Qinggan Jueze [China Can Say No: Political and Emotional Choices in the Post—Cold War Era]*. Beijing: Zhonghua Gongshang Lianhe Chubanshe.

Stockard, Janice E. 1989. *Daughters of the Canton Delta: Marriage Patterns and Economic Strategies in South China, 1860–1930*. Stanford: Stanford University Press.

Strand, David. 1989. *Rickshaw Beijing: City People and Politics in the 1920s*. Berkeley: University of California Press.

Suzuki, Seichiro. 1978 [1934]. *Taiwan Jiuguan Xisu Xinyang [Old Customs and Traditional Beliefs of Taiwan]*. Trans. Gao Jianzhi and Feng Zuomin. Taipei: Zhongwen.

Taiwan Sheng Wenxian Weiyuanhui, comp. 1980. *Taiwan Sheng Tongzhi [Complete Gazetteer of Taiwan Province]*. Taipei: Zhongwen.

Tang Zhenchang. 1995. "Civil Consciousness and Shanghai Society." *Social Sciences in China* (Spring):58–73.

Tan Hong. 1986. "'Orientalism' and Image-making: Chinese Americans as 'Sojourner' and 'Model Minority.'" Durham, N.C.: unpublished.

Taussig, Michael T. 1980. *The Devil and Commodity Fetishism in South America*. Chapel Hill, N.C.: University of North Carolina Press.

Thomas, Keith. 1983. *Man and the Natural World: A History of the Modern Sensibility*. New York: Pantheon.

Thompson, E. P. 1971. "The Moral Economy of the English Crowd in the Eighteenth Century." *Past and Present* 50:76–136.

Tien, Hung-mao. 1989. *The Great Transition: Political and Social Change in the Republic of China*. Stanford: Hoover Institution Press.

Tien, Hung-mao, and Tun-jen Cheng. 1997. "Crafting Democratic Institutions in Taiwan." *China Journal* 37:1–27.

Topley, Marjorie. 1975. "Marriage Resistance in Rural Kwangtung." In Margery Wolf and Roxane Witke, eds., *Women in Chinese Society*, 67–88. Stanford: Stanford University Press.

Tsai, Kellee S. 1998. "A Circle of Friends, a Web of Trouble: Rotating Credit Associations in China." *Harvard China Review* 1(1):81–83.

Tsai Ming-hui, and Chang Mau-kuei. 1994. "Formation and Transformation of Local *P'ai-hsi*: A Case Study of Ho-k'ou Town." *Bulletin of the Institute of Ethnology, Academia Sinica* 77:125–156.

Unger, Jonathan. 1996. "'Bridges': Private Business, the Chinese Government and the Rise of New Associations." *China Quarterly* 147:795–819.

Verdery, Katherine. 1991. "Theorizing Socialism: A Prologue to the 'Transition.'" *American Ethnologist* 18(3):419–439.

Wakeman, Frederic. 1993. "The Civil Society and Public Sphere Debate: Western Reflections on Chinese Political Culture." *Modern China* 19(2):108–138.

Walker, Kathy Le Mons. 1993. "Economic Growth, Peasant Marginalization, and the Sexual Division of Labor in Early Twentieth-century China: Women's Work in Nantong County." *Modern China* 19(3):354–386.

Wallerstein, Immanuel. 1990. "Culture as the Ideological Battleground of the Modern World-system." *Theory, Culture & Society* 7:31–55.

Wang, Juju Chin-Shou. 1998. "Economic Growth with Pollution: Taiwan's Environmental Experience." In Uday Desai, ed., *Ecological Policy and Politics in Developing Countries: Economic Growth, Democracy, and Environment*, 121–151. Albany, N.Y.: State University of New York Press.

Wang, Xu. 1997. "Mutual Empowerment of State and Peasantry: Grassroots Democracy in Rural China." *World Development* 25(9):1431–1442.

Wank, David L. 1995. "Private Business, Bureaucracy, and Political Alliance in a Chinese City." *Australian Journal of Chinese Affairs* 33:55–71.

Watson, James L. 1985. "Standardizing the Gods: The Promotion of T'ien Hou ('Empress of Heaven') Along the South China Coast, 960–1960." In David Johnson, Andrew J. Nathan, and Evelyn S. Rawski, eds., *Popular Culture in Late Imperial China*, 292–324. Berkeley: University of California Press.

Waylen, G. 1994. "Women and Democratization: Conceptualizing Gender Relations in Transition Politics." *World Politics* 46:327–354.

Weber, Max. 1946. "The Protestant Sects and the Spirit of Capitalism." In H. H. Gerth and C. Wright Mills, eds., *From Max Weber: Essays in Sociology*, 302–322. New York: Oxford University Press.

———. 1951. *The Religion of China: Confucianism and Taoism*. Ed. and trans. Hans H. Gerth. Intro. by C. K. Yang. New York: Free Press.

———. 1958. *The Protestant Ethic and the Spirit of Capitalism*. Trans. Talcott Parsons. Foreword by R. H. Tawney. New York: Scribner's.

Weller, Robert P. 1984. "Ideology, Organization and Rebellion in Chinese Sectarian Religion." In Janos M. Bak and Gerhard Benecke, eds., *Religion and Rural Revolt*, 390–406. Manchester: Manchester University Press.

———. 1987. *Unities and Diversities in Chinese Religion*. Seattle: University of Washington.

———. 1994. *Resistance, Chaos and Control in China: Taiping Rebels, Taiwanese Ghosts and Tiananmen*. London: Macmillan.

Weller, Robert P., and Peter K. Bol. 1998. "From Heaven-and-Earth to Nature: Chinese Concepts of the Environment and Their Influence on Policy Implementation." In Mary Evelyn Tucker and John Berthrong, eds., *Confucianism and Ecology: The Interrelation of Heaven, Earth, and Humans*, 313–341. Cambridge, Mass.: Harvard University Center for the Study of World Religions.

Weller, Robert P., and Hsin-Huang Michael Hsiao. 1998. "Culture, Gender and Community in Taiwan's Environmental Movement." In Arne Kalland and Gerard Persoon, eds., *Environmental Movements in Asia*, 83–109. Surrey: Curzon.

White, Jenny B. 1996. "Civic Culture and Islam in Urban Turkey." In Chris Hann and Elizabeth Dunn, eds., *Civil Society: Challenging Western Notions*, 143–154. London: Routledge.

Winckler, Edwin A. 1994. "Cultural Policy on Postwar Taiwan." In Stevan Harrell and Huang Chün-chieh, eds., *Cultural Change in Postwar Taiwan*. Boulder: Westview Press.

Winn, Jane Kaufman. 1994. "Not by Rule of Law: Mediating State-Society Relations in Taiwan Through the Underground Economy." In Murray A. Rubenstein, ed., *The Other Taiwan: 1945 to the Present*, 183–214. New York: M. E. Sharpe.

Wolf, Eric R. 1966. *Peasants*. Englewood Cliffs, N.J.: Prentice-Hall.

Wolf, Margery. 1972. *Women and the Family in Rural Taiwan*. Stanford: Stanford University Press.

———. 1985. *Revolution Postponed: Women in Contemporary China*. Stanford: Stanford University Press.

Wong, John. 1996. "Promoting Confucianism for Socioeconomic Development: The Singapore Experience." In Wei-ming Tu, ed., *Confucian Traditions in East Asian Modernity*, 277–293. Cambridge, Mass.: Harvard University Press.

Yan, Yunxiang. 1996. *The Flow of Gifts: Reciprocity and Social Networks in a Chinese Village*. Stanford: Stanford University Press.

Yang Kuo-shu, and Cheng Po-shyun. 1987. "Chuantong Jiazhiguan, Geren Xiandaixing ji Zuzhi Xingwei: Hourujia Jiashou de Yixiang Weiguan Yanzheng [Confucianized Values, Individual Modernity, and Organizational Behavior: An Empirical Test of the Post-Confucian Hypothesis]." *Bulletin of the Institute of Ethnology, Academia Sinica* 64:1–49.

Yang, Mayfair Mei-hui. 1994. *Gifts, Favors and Banquets: The Art of Social Relationships in China*. Ithaca: Cornell University Press.

Yu Yingshi. 1987. *Zhongguo Jinshi Zongjiao Lunli Yu Shangren Jingshen [Modern Chinese Religious Ethics and Business Spirit]*. Taipei: Lunjing.

Zhang Maogui. 1990. *Shehui Yundong yu Zhengzhi Zhuanhua [Social Movements and Political Change]*. Taipei: Guojia Zhengce Yanjiu Ziliao Zhongxin.

Zhang Wei'an. 1996. "Fuojiao Ciji Gongde Hui yu Ziyuan Huishou [The Buddhist Compassion Merit Society and Recycling]." Paper presented at the Workshop on Culture, Media and Society in Contemporary Taiwan. Harvard University.

Zhao Dingjun. 1992. "Yiguan Dao Caili Shen Bu Ke Ce [The Immeasurable Wealth of the Yiguan Dao]." *Wealth Magazine* 121 (April):131.

Zheng Zhiming. 1987. "Youji Lei Luanshu Suo Xianshi zhi Zongjiao Xin Qushi [The New Trend in Religious Worship as Seen from Biographical Travels, Memoirs]." *Bulletin of the Institute of Ethnology, Academia Sinica* (61):105–127.

Index

Surname associations, 30–31, 32–33,
57, 109
Sutra singing groups, 34

Taipei, 7, 114, 121
business in, 68
Taiwan, 1, 2–3, 31–32, 57, 58, 128,
147(n3)
and Asian financial crisis, 79(n19)
authoritarianism in, 45–50
Buddhism in, 96–100, 104(n35)
business in, 63, 66–68, 69–70, 74,
76–77
and civil society, 16
and Confucianism, 9–10
and corporatism, 45–47
and culture, 11–12
environmentalism in, 6–7, 16–17,
111–125, 127
geomancy in, 56
ghost worship in, 47–50, 90, 91,
101, 108
and political change, 6–7, 11–12,
135–147
religion in, 83–85, 87–88, 89–102
and social action, 107–125, 131
social ties in, 43
and voluntary associations, 12, 14
women in, 17, 34–35, 72, 93–100,
101–102, 104(n35), 113–114,
119–120, 140–142
Taiwan Environmental Protection
Agency, 125
Taiwan Environmental Protection
Union (TEPU), 112, 113, 127
Taiwan Greenpeace, 112
Taiwan Power, 118
Taiwan Strait, 76, 127
Taussig, Michael, 9
Temple religion, 83, 84–88, 101,
102(n1), 102(n3), 103(n7). *See also*
Rituals; Temples
Temples, 29, 50, 108–109
and environmentalism, 115–118
and village connections, 31–32
and women, 33
See also Rituals; Temple religion

TEPU. *See* Taiwan Environmental
Protection Union
Thoreau, Henry David, 111–112
Three Gorges dam project, 127
Three obediences, 33
Tiananmen demonstrations, 128
Tianjin, 72–73, 74, 80(n37)
Tibet, 3
Ties, social, 52–53
and local elites, 29–31
and village connections, 31–33
and women, 33–35, 36, 38(n24)
See also Networks; Social networks
Time, 6
Timidity, 78(n7)
Tocqueville, 13
and civil society, 14
Tong ("same") ties, 30–31
Tong xiang (same native place), 30–31,
57, 109
Tong xing (same surname), 30–31,
32–33, 57, 109
Tong xue (same study), 30
Totalitarian project, 42–43, 51
Travel, 72
Trust, 5–6, 22(n46), 72
and credit, 67
and social ties, 23–36
and voluntary associations, 13

Unions, 57, 126
United States, 143
Universal liberal culture, vs.
authoritarianism, 1–3
Universal Salvation, festival of,
47–50
University libraries, 55
UN World Conference on Human
Rights (1993), 4
Upright officials, 69
Urban street committees, 109
Utilitarianism, 89

Values, Western vs. Eastern, 4
Vegetarianism, 92
Vietnam, 96
Village committees, 109